TENNIS

GUIDE TO MASTERING YOUR GAME - STRATEGIES, EQUIPMENT, AND DRILLS TO BECOMING A COMPLETE TENNIS PLAYER.

BY: PETER WILLIAMS

© Copyright 2016 - All rights reserved.

In no way is it legal to reproduce, duplicate, or transmit any part of this document in either electronic means or in printed format. Recording of this publication is strictly prohibited and any storage of this document is not allowed unless with written permission from the publisher. All rights reserved.

The information provided herein is stated to be truthful and consistent, in that any liability, in terms of inattention or otherwise, by any usage or abuse of any policies, processes, or directions contained within is the solitary and utter responsibility of the recipient reader. Under no circumstances will any legal responsibility or blame be held against the publisher for any reparation, damages, or monetary loss due to the information herein, either directly or indirectly.

Respective authors own all copyrights not held by the publisher.

Legal Notice:

This book is copyright protected. This is only for personal use. You cannot amend, distribute, sell, use, quote or paraphrase any part or the content within this book without the consent of the author or copyright owner. Legal action will be pursued if this is breached.

Disclaimer Notice:

Please note the information contained within this document is for educational and entertainment purposes only. Every attempt has been made to provide accurate, up to date and reliable complete information. No warranties of any kind are expressed or implied. Readers acknowledge that the author is not engaging in the rendering of legal, financial, medical or professional advice.

By reading this document, the reader agrees that under no circumstances are we responsible for any losses, direct or indirect, which are incurred as a result of the use of information contained within this document, including, but not limited to, —errors, omissions, or inaccuracies.

Free Bonus: Get 40% OFF All Of Our Products On Amazon!!

Coupon Code: 21KSport

Checkout Our Tennis Products

http://amzn.to/2fejZeo

http://amzn.to/2fegXXw

TABLE OF CONTENTS

Introduction 9
Chapter One Fundamentals Of The Game 11
Chapter Two Learning How to Keep Score 19
Chapter Three The Rules of the Game 25
Chapter Four Skills and Techniques Required for Tennis 27
Chapter Five Learn the Groundstrokes 35
Chapter Six How to Serve 47
Chapter Seven How to Volley and Drills for Improving Your Volley 55
Chapter Eight How to Play the Overhead 63
Chapter Nine What Beginners Need To Know 71
Chapter Ten Some Exercises for Beginners 79
Chapter Eleven Advanced Strategies 89
Chapter Twelve Single Player Strategies 97
Chapter Thirteen Double Player Strategies 103
Chapter Fourteen Equipment Considerations 111
Chapter Fifteen Tennis Psychology 121
Chapter Sixteen Drill Exercises 129
Conclusion 137

INTRODUCTION

When people think of 'tennis' the obvious association is going to be a rigorous sport whose full range of skills, hard work, and dedication is exemplified by some of the nationally acclaimed tournaments such as Wimbledon. Now, whether you're a professional tennis player and athlete aiming to increase your skills and get that extra edge over your opponents, or you're a newcomer to the sport of tennis and just getting into the game for the very first time, there are a number of fundamental skills, drills, and equipment that are common to both. This manual aims to encourage players of all levels by giving them suggestions and tips to improve their game, as well as to minimize errors or bad habits.

Such things include different strategies related to single versus double player tennis, exercises that are proven to help and increase focus, dexterity, and stamina, and personal choices about the quality and usefulness of current equipment on the market such as dampeners and racket styles. By the end, we hope to have not only improved your understanding of some of the more intricate nuances of tennis, but also hopefully motivated you to integrate these techniques into your own playing.

10 | TENNIS

CHAPTER ONE
FUNDAMENTALS OF THE GAME

The first thing you need to do when you start out with the game of tennis is to comprehend and familiarize yourself with its decidedly strange scoring technique. Since you are a tennis novice, you should first know the way of keeping track of who's winning. Scoring doesn't begin with 1 or 0. It begins with the expression "love", which basically means zero. The first point that a player gets is 15, then 30 and then 40. The point that comes after 40 is the point that wins the game. It's called match point or game point or set point. The term depends upon whether the point wins the set, the match or the game.

The Score

The server's score is constantly declared first. In this way, for example if the server has won two points and his rival, the recipient, has none, the declared score would be 30-love. In the event that in a game there is a tie at 40-40, it is known as "deuce". In case the server gets the following point, the term used is server advantage; however, in case the receiver gets the following point, the term used is receiver advantage. The term 'advantage' is used in light of the fact that the player who has it just needs to get one more point in order to win. If the player with the advantage does not get this one point the game backtracks to deuce. The scoring is maybe somewhat complex. However, it is important to comprehend as you figure out how to play the game.

The Tennis Court

Now that we've understood basic scoring, the next step to become skilled at as a tennis novice is to understand the court. The length of a tennis court is 78 feet and its breadth is 27 feet. The court is isolated into equal parts by the net length-wise. At every end of the court, you will find white baselines. This is where the serves are taken. These baselines are additionally the lines outside the field of play. A ball must not ricochet past them or it's considered out. This means that a point is lost for whichever player hit the ball.

There are two white imprints on each side. These show the width meant to be used for singles play with the bigger width meant for when you're playing doubles. The service court is marked by the short white line that extends halfway down from the net. As a tennis novice, you can't figure out how to play the game without comprehending these guidelines. With sufficient practice time chipping away at tennis strokes, a player may find that the right tennis procedures might be in certainty a component that can advance him or her, permitting them to hit shots that they wouldn't have been able to with their old and wasteful tennis strokes. Obviously, this means that you can improve all your strokes in the game. The tennis serve, forehand and backhand are the three greatest tennis strokes in the present day tennis. Every one of the tennis strokes additionally require you to know good techniques so that they work efficiently for you.

Tennis Singles

Since you comprehend the court, we should figure out how you can play tennis with a few specifics. As I have already said, a tennis amateur can play a singles or doubles match maybe a couple players on either side of the net. A serve taken from behind what is known as the baseline is what starts each game, and, in fact, each point too. You must ensure that the ball bounces on opposite side of the service court and it must do so diagonally across from you. (You may find that the serve is the most difficult stroke to play at first.) The point or play proceeds until one player is unable to hit the ball back or instead hits it outside the field of play.

I've invested years in endeavors to comprehend tennis strategies and privileged insights that few individuals ever learn in lessons. Most junior tennis players who play competitively have the benefit of money and time to create and study tennis strategies, yet perhaps you don't. Tennis procedures are an imperative part for each tennis player. The smallest changes in technique can bring about huge enhancements.

Learn How to Serve

Along these lines, as you have learnt now, if you want to learn to play tennis, it is very important for you to know how to serve. Here's how you need to do it (for right-handed players — if you are a left-handed player you ought to turn around the directions): When you position yourself, both your feet should be behind the baseline. Position yourself sideways so that your left foot is pointed towards the right hand net post. Make sure that you are holding the ball in your left hand. Then, raise your left hand and toss the ball up in the air. The toss should be about one foot high and positioned in front of your left foot. It should also be above your reach by about 18 inches. With the ball still in the air, you need to make a back and up movement with your racket. When you hit the ball make sure you are stretched to your full reach. Your racket arm should be straight and at the most elevated point conceivable. You are exchanging your weight to your front foot from your back foot so that your shot has added strength.

The movement as you hit the ball should be an "up and over" one as though you were tossing the racket at the ball. Once you have hit the ball, finish your swing. The finish will push you forward further into the court, ensuring that you are ready to hit the shot when it is returned. Great! You're advancing admirably in your endeavors! In case you don't like how you have served — maybe you end up missing the ball during the swing — don't stress; this is quite common when you're starting out.

Tennis Doubles

Yet, what if it's a doubles match? How would I figure out how to play the game then, you ponder?! Who will serve? When playing doubles, the turn to serve keeps changing. For example, if there are two teams with A and B in one team playing against C and D in the other team, the first serve goes to A and after that it would go to C and afterward back to B and lastly to D.

Likewise, something else you should know when you fathom how to play tennis is this: When the odd-numbered games in a set, including the principal game, come to an end, the players will need to move to the opposite end of the court from where they started. This is valid in both doubles and singles matches.

Other points you have to know as you figure out how to play

All things considered, as you figure out how to play, you have to discern how you need to proceed with the play. When the serve works out, the game may proceed with an assortment of shots. Regularly, play will proceed with groundstrokes. A groundstroke is a shot that is taken post the ball bouncing once. It can be hit one of two ways: with a backhand or a forehand stroke. In the forehand stroke, the face of the racket connects with the ball, with the palm of your hand confronting the ball. In the backhand stroke, the reverse side of the racket connects with the ball. Your palm will need to be facing away from the ball. You'll need to learn both forehand and backhand shots if you want to learn to play tennis effectively.

Tennis strategies have adjusted for each new era of tennis players. The forehand method has developed, from old fashioned closed positions, to rotational angular force hitting styles.

Play tennis with a forehand stroke

Start with the grip. The eastern forehand grip is the most well-known hold in tennis; it is additionally the best option as you figure out how to play this game. You need to utilize it for both your forehand drive and the greater part of the shots you play.

Put your hand on the racket strings while keeping it flat, and afterward slide it down to the handle. Then your fingers need to be wrapped around the racket. Your first finger ought to be forward marginally as though you were holding the trigger of a weapon. Keep your fingers loose and devoid of tension. The eastern forehand grip is frequently called the "shake hands" hold by the individuals who have quite recently started to figure out how to play, in light of the fact that, basically, it seems as though you are shaking hands. For the vast majority, it is the favored grip for serving — especially, when you first figure out how to play.

Tennis Backhand Stroke

Once more, start with the grip. Whether you utilize a one handed backhand stroke or a two handed backhand stroke, it's imperative to grip the racket nearer to the upper bevel with the hand that is dominant. For a two handed backhand stroke, the hand that isn't dominant ought to grasp underneath the handle, and your palm should be laid solidly on the handle of the racket. Fingers need to be tension-free, and not very near one another. The grip for the two handed stroke ought to have your non-dominant hand adjoining the first. It's important to rehearse both the strokes as you figure out how to play tennis.

Picking the Right Equipment

At last, picking the right gear is crucial in your learning. Appropriate grip measure means that you don't suffer unnecessary pain. You need to hold your racket hand out. Keep the palm side up. You need to measure from the tip of the ring finger to the wrinkle of the ring finger. This tells you the right grip estimate. This ought to be the estimation around the handle of your racket, with the diameter being by and large around four inches across.

Indeed, even your selection of socks, shoes, and other clothes are vital contemplations when you are in the process of learning the game. Instead of running shoes, you should use tennis shoes as they are manufactured to deal with a side-to-side motion. They ought to have a herringbone tread. This results in longer enduring assurance and grip. Socks ought to be ready to retain sweat and thick, thus helping you avoid conditions such as athlete's foot. By and large, tennis apparel is white; shading that keeps the player cool because it reflects the sun's heat. (Notwithstanding when you are simply starting to figure out how to play tennis Wear the proper gear!)

A Lifelong Sport

In the event that you learn how to play, this can become your initial move toward a lifetime of wellness and joy. What's more, now that we've examined how to figure out how to play with the fundamentals, you're prepared to go on the court. There's no better approach to figure out how to play than with practice; practice ensures that you'll not just figure out how to play the game, you'll know how to play it well.

CHAPTER TWO
LEARNING HOW TO KEEP SCORE

It is true that one of the weirdest scoring frameworks in the sporting scene is utilized by tennis. Yet it is ostensibly a standout amongst the best games to play. Once you take in the scoring framework, you won't experience serious difficulties with it. Look down to Step 1 to take in the scoring framework in the sport of tennis.

1. Consider the distinction between a set, a game and a match. The entire playing time of tennis is referred to as a match. Depending upon which league you are in, you will need to play the best of three or five sets in a match. Six games constitute a set. Best out of these six wins the set.

2. Learn how to score each game. In each game, one player serves. You win the game when you or your team (in case you're playing doubles) wins four points. When the ball is served by one player, and the adversary hits the ball back a point is begun. The point goes on in a forward and backward way until one of the players hits it into the net or out of the

court. There are times that the game can take seven or more points to be over. This will generally happen if one player has won four points while the other one has won three. For each player, every point has a value of its own:

- "15 points" is the first point won

- "30 points" is the second point won

- "40 points" is the third point won

- GAME (that means the end of the game) is made by the fourth point won

3. When you serve, know how you need to call out the score. During every game, the server needs to call out the score loudly enough that the rival can hear it (If you play in an expert setting they have a score attendant). You are constantly expected to say your score, trailed by your adversary's score. For instance:

- You would call out "30-15" in case you have won two points and your rival has won one.

- You would call out "15-40", in case your rival has won three points and you have won one.

4. See how every to score every set. You play each set until one team or player wins six games. You should call out the

number of games won by every team or player, beginning with your score, when you start to serve. For instance:

- In the event that four games have been won by you, and two by your adversary, you need to call out "4-2". This should be done prior to beginning your "service game" (the game in which you serve rather than receive the ball).

5. If there is a tie, understand that you need to win by two. This alludes to both sets and games. Below are a few cases:

- In the event that the score is 40 to 40 for both, to be able to win the game you need to win two points one after another.

- In the event the score is 5 to 5 and 5 games have been won by both of you, so as to win the set, two more games need to be won by you consecutively to make the score 7-5.

- In the event that 5 to 5 is the score and the following game has been won by you, 6-5 becomes the new score. In the event that the following game is won by your opponent and 6-6 is the score, to be able to win the set, you should win 8 to 6. A few sets have seen scores of 12 to 10 or significantly higher.

6. Know when you've won or lost the match. You will either need to win two out of three sets or three out of five sets, depending on the league you belong to. In any case, as with sets and games, you should win by two. What this can mean is that in the event that you and your adversary continue tying matches can now and then be seven out of nine sets or five out of seven sets.

7. After the match know how to record the score. You ought to note down the score of every set on a scorecard. Make sure to first write your score. For instance, in the event that you were the winner of the match, this is what your scorecard may resemble:

4-6, 6-2, 6-3. What this means is that you lost the first set 4 games to 6; you won the second set 6 games to 2; and the third set was won by you 6 games to 3.

Understanding the Terms Used

1. Comprehend what "all" signifies in tennis. "All" essentially signifies "both" in tennis jargon. In the event that your adversary and you have each won one point, 15-15 being the score, "15-all" would be what you would call out. The same applies to sets. In case both of you have won three games, before starting your serve, you would need to call out "3-all".

2. Recognize what "love" implies. No, this does not mean the sentimental, or even the dispassionate, type of love. "Love" alludes to a score of zero in tennis. For instance:

   - You need to call out "love-30", in case you serve and haven't won any points yet, however your adversary has won two.

   - The same applies to games. You would call out "3-love", in case three games have been won by you, but none by your adversary.

   - You would call out "love-all", in case, you are simply beginning a game and no points have been won by either of you.

3. Comprehend the words "deuce" and 'advantage'. In tennis, a 'deuce' occurs when there is a tied score of 40 to 40 between two players during a game. You can play out a deuce in one of two ways – either the person who gets the following point wins, or "advantage" ('ad' for short) is played. This implies that the deuce point and the following point must be won by a player.

4. Distinguish between 'ad-in' and 'ad-out'. The score is considered 'ad-in' (advantage-in, this means that the advantage is to the server) at the point that the player who is

23 | TENNIS

serving ends up winning the deuce point. The score is considered 'ad-out', at the point the deuce point is won by the receiver. The score becomes deuce again, in the event the deuce point is won by a player, yet that player doesn't win the ad.

CHAPTER THREE

THE RULES OF THE GAME

Guidelines of Tennis

The toss of a coin begins the game to decide which of the two (or four) players will first serve and what side they will be serving from.

Then each point has to be served by the server from different sides upon the baseline. The server's feet should never cross the baseline before serving.

In case the server is unable to play his or her first serve properly, a second serve may be taken advantage of. In case however he or she is unable to play his or her second serve, the point is lost after a 'double fault' has been called.

In case the ball touches the top of the net during the serve but then goes into the service area, a call of 'still then let' is made and the server gets the chance to serve again without incurring any penalty. In the event that the server hits the ball into the net but the ball doesn't go into the area of service, the server loses that serve and a call of out is made.

The recipient can stand wherever he or she pleases when returning the serve. However, if he or she strikes the ball before it has bounced, the server gets the point.

There is no limit to the number of shots that the players can play between them, once the ball has been served. A player wins the point when the ball is struck in such a way that the opponent cannot return it within the scoring ranges.

A player has to win 6 games by at least 2 to win the set. There won't be a tie breaker in the last set. It means that the players must win by 2 games without any limits.

In case a player diverts his rival, comes into contact with the net, or blocks in any case then he or she loses the point automatically.

For the point to be called in, any part of the line can be hit by the ball. Once the ball falls outside though, it is out.

After 6 games the balls in a tennis match must be changed and new balls brought in.

In the event that he or she is unable to strike the ball back in the right ranges on the court, the ball hits the net but doesn't go into the rival's region or the player is unable to strike the ball back before the ball bounces twice while it is in his or her area, a player loses a point.

CHAPTER FOUR
SKILLS AND TECHNIQUES REQUIRED FOR TENNIS

Tennis aptitudes and methods identify with the specialized, mental and physical abilities and capacities that a player has. These key tennis aptitudes and procedures are fundamental so that players can achieve a world class tennis level.

Tennis Techniques and Skills are fundamental in the improvement of a tennis player's amusement

Tennis is the sort of game that requires a considerable measure of aptitudes and techniques. To get to the top, a player must have the specialized, mental, and physical aptitudes and systems. An expanded array of tennis abilities and strategies are required in case a tennis player wants to improve his or her game.

Players need to have an extensive variety of various tennis abilities and techniques that include stroke generation, methodology, mental durability, and an athletic physicality. Some of these aptitudes and strategies are talked about here.

Major Techniques and Skills

The following are the major tennis specialized aptitudes that each beginner player ought to obtain. Additional aptitudes are obtained as players develop and turn out to be more proficient at the more advanced specialized abilities. Cases of these superior abilities are net charge, net play, making contact, cut, swing, drop shots and numerous others. Just the principal tennis abilities and systems are portrayed here.

Forehand Techniques and Skills

The forehand stroke is the main piece of tennis abilities and strategies for a lot of players whether they are beginners or professionals. It is considered the most habitual stroke in the game.

In case you happen to be right-handed, and your adversary gives back a ball directly at your body, your inclination is to venture to the left side. You hit from the right half of your body. In case you happen to be left-handed, and your rival gives back a point directly at your body, you habitually venture to your right and hit from the left half of your body.

Since the forehand is a kind of characteristic stroke, it is used more often by players when contrasted with alternate strokes.

Backhand Techniques and skills

The backhand is made from the side opposite to the forehand. As such, in the event that you are right-handed, when you hit the ball you do so from the left half of your body. In case you are left-handed, when you hit the ball you do it from the right half of your body.

To accurately carry out the backhand, you need to bring the hand that is dominant or the racket hand around your body prior to hitting the ball.

It can be cumbersome to execute a backhand at first. However, in case you persevere and hone it frequently, the backhand can be a decent additional instrument for your aptitudes and techniques.

Serve Techniques and skills

In a game the beginning of a point is the tennis serve. The player who serves is known as the server. The player on the flip side is the recipient. There are a few sorts of serves, for example, topspin, topspin-cut, level, cut, kick and numerous others.

Because each point is begun by the serve, it's vital to build up this among different tennis abilities and methods.

An impeccable serve is accomplished by getting the right position, the right serve grip and the right toss of the ball. In addition, if the server can execute the correct body motions (body coiling and knee bending), the correct point of contact and the correct racket swing power can likewise be added. Above all, the serve needs to be produced as an essential weapon while achieving depth and precision.

Tennis Lob

A lob shot is a critical additional benefit that can be added to a player's aptitudes and strategies. It can be utilized as a hostile or guarded shot. A lob shot is carried out by hitting the ball deep and high into your adversary's court. Normally, you hit a hostile lob shot when the adversary is near the net. At the same time, you use the defensive lob shot to drive the adversary back and permit you to recoup to a superior protective position. Accordingly, you can regain control of the game and use it to your advantage.

Overhead

An overhead is a shot that is hit over the player's head similar to the execution of the serve. It is likewise known as a smash shot because usually power goes into the hit. In the event that it is done correctly, it garners a point for the smasher. While you normally hit a lob shot down deep, you normally hit an overhead shot close to the net or amidst the court. Now and again, an opponent can return a bad lob shot (not high and not very deep) as an overhead shot. So that an overhead shot has more power, you need to hit it before the ball bounces. A lob shot is another enhancement to the player's abilities and techniques that guarantees a point.

Volley

A volley is a shot in which the ball is hit before it ricochets on the ground. This does not include the serve and the overhead shot. In many cases, you hit a volley when playing net. Depending on the conditions it should likewise be possible regardless of the possibility that you are in the center or even on the baseline.

It is considered a feature of the overall abilities and techniques that you can apply when shaky or not in the position to hit a groundstroke. Be that as it may, you normally play it as a hostile shot close to the net.

Physical Techniques and skills

The sport of tennis requires a great deal of physical exercises. It needs nimbleness, speed, adaptability and endurance if you want to reach the top. These are among abilities and strategies that you need to be an effective player.

You require speed to keep running for the ball as fast as could be allowed and you require readiness and sharpness to envision your rival's shot.

Your ligaments and muscles should be adaptable so that you have the capacity to strike balls that appear to be inaccessible. In conclusion, you need the staying power to keep going for long periods of time of matches.

Balance

One of the critical physical aptitudes and techniques a player needs to have is balance. Balance is imperative to hit exact and well placed shots. Great balance additionally minimizes injuries, especially those that occur in the lower part of the body, for example, the legs, lower legs and knees. Drills and exercises to enhance balance should be possible both on and off-court (e.g. in a gym).

Dexterity

Tennis is a game in which dexterity is vital in order for your hand and alternate parts of your body to rapidly respond to move the right way according to what is seen by your eyes. Dexterity is one of a large number of aptitudes and techniques that are vital, especially for advanced tennis in which the way of the game is snappy and quick. In spite of the fact that it is believed that this ability develops through years of playing, drills to build up this aptitude are still important especially for youthful novices.

Mental Techniques and Skills
Motivation

Tennis aptitudes and strategies are of no use without motivation. Being motivated enought to fulfill something is the formula of numerous fruitful individuals in their own fields.

This is also valid for tennis players. Youthful beginners need to have motivation to take in the diverse tennis aptitudes and strategies for them to do well and move forward. Proficient players on the other hand, must be motivated enough to win troublesome matches.

Concentration

Focus and concentration assume a key part in each tennis player's execution. To be focused while on court implies you need to get rid of all alternate considerations, especially anything negative that can occupy you. You need to concentrate so that you can get your first serve in especially during significant points. Otherwise you have to focus so that you don't miss your second serve to keep away from double faults.

Focus is imperative on court as well as off court also, for example, during practice. You need full focus so that you can enhance your tennis abilities and techniques during standard practice.

Spirit of Competition

Tennis is an intense game especially for those playing singles. It can get to be harder if the match is going against you since you are separate from everyone else out there on court. Your competitive spirit is tried when you play against the leading adversary. How you handle the circumstance when you are losing will be determined based on your competitive spirit. A focused player refuses to surrender until the winner has been proclaimed.

Critical thinking

A player must build up a course of action depending on whoever his or her rival will be. Be that as it may, a course of action does not work every time. Dissimilar to basketball in which a mentor can request a time out to alter his or her course of action in case the first is not working, a tennis player has to think of his or her own answers in the event that his or her strategies are unsuccessful.

CHAPTER FIVE
LEARN THE GROUNDSTROKES

Tennis For Beginners – 5 Steps To Consistent Groundstrokes

At the point when a tennis learner begins figuring out how to play tennis, they initially need to learn essential forehand and strike procedure as these will permit them to play, appreciate the game and return for more.learn-how-to-play-tennis

The fundamentals of tennis obviously additionally incorporate the serve, volley and the overhead strokes, yet these strategies can be adapted later as the fledgling figures out how to rally first helpfully with their accomplice.

All groundstrokes, which means the forehand and the one-gave or two-gave strike variety, take after fundamentally the same as well ordered movements with just slight conformities between them.

The accompanying directions for tennis amateurs will assemble a legitimate establishment of essential strokes and permit them to figure out how to play tennis in the speediest way that is available.

5 Steps To Learning Tennis Technique For Beginners

beginner1Since ball judgment is not grew yet with amateurs, tennis first must be played at a shorter separation and at a lower speed. We call it small scale tennis, and it's played from simply behind the administration line.

Playing at such a short separation and low speed permits tenderfoots to at present have sufficient energy to judge the ball genuinely well and not feel surged as it contacts them. It's additionally basic that, since we altered the tennis game surely, we adjust stroke method, as well.

A standout amongst the most widely recognized slip-ups when figuring out how to play tennis is taking in the fundamental groundstroke strategy from the begin, which implies that the player is being instructed to make a full turn and execute a full swing at the ball.

This essentially makes an abundant excess power and swing velocity and makes it hard to control the ball well at such a short separation. In this way we need to utilize particular tennis directions for amateurs with a specific end goal to show them to play tennis right from the principal moment they're on the court.

By taking after these 5 well ordered lessons for tennis fledglings, they will have the capacity to advance rapidly and in the meantime make the most of their time on the court.

1. Playing from the Contact Point and Extending Forward

step by step instructions to play-forehandInstead of educating the planning of strokes first with a full turn and the backswing, we really put the racquet only marginally behind the normal contact point.

You may feel that you have no power there, yet you'll rapidly understand that notwithstanding moving the racquet only a couple inches towards the ball as you're going to hit it gives it enough vitality to fly over the net and achieve your accomplice after one bob.

Hitting the ball at the ideal time and at the right contact indicate is the key consistency and right tennis strategy. Concentrating first on this component of the game as opposed to on the mechanics of the stroke will help each tennis novice enhance rapidly and have the capacity to play without numerous slip-ups.

In this initial step, you don't need to concentrate much on the complete system; rather, you basically augment your arm forward, directing the ball towards the opposite side.

This underlying specialized modification applies to the forehand, one-gave strike and the two-gave strike.

In all cases, they begin playing from the contact point first and essentially expand straight forward and upwards, giving the ball some bearing and tallness.

2. Playing from the Contact Point and Adding a Follow-through

forehand-take after throughAs you turn out to be more agreeable and steady playing from the contact point and stretching out forward, we can include the essential finish system.

On the forehand and two-gave strike groundstrokes, the complete is the same: we complete with the racquet over the shoulder. It ought to touch the shoulder with the edge and point its butt top towards the net.

In the event of a one-gave strike, the body needs to remain sideways with the arm completely developed and the racquet in a vertical position with its butt top indicating the ground.

You ought to now continue playing smaller than normal tennis, as yet setting up your strokes by putting the racquet simply behind the contact point and now including the finish method every stroke with the goal that you begin imbuing this development into your subliminal.

These two stages are imperative for the initial couple of lessons that a tennis amateur takes as they concentrate on the most vital and really a standout amongst the most difficult parts of tennis, which is meeting the ball at a perfect separation from the body. This is the most proficient and agreeable approach to play tennis.

Just when the player turns out to be more predictable playing small scale tennis with this changed stroke system do we move to the following movement in creating essential groundstroke method.

3. Including the Split Step

A split stride is the fundamental sort of footwork that should be available on each shot you're getting.

It's a snappy bounce where you hop marginally off the ground and split your feet wide noticeable all around and arrive in this same position, to be specific with your feet well separated. That helps you push off in any bearing rapidly.

The key for the split stride is legitimate planning and that implies that you should arrive into the split stride precisely when you understand where the ball is going. In the event that you time it accurately, you'll additionally feel that you can move dangerously towards the ball.

4. Expanding the Distance of Play and Adding Stroke Preparation

Before expanding the separation to the full court, a tennis fledgling ought to play for some time at about ¾ remove from the net, implying that they move simply inside the benchmark and point their shots at their adversary's administration line range.

This still keeps the speed of the ball low and gives them enough time to judge the ball well and move to it without being surged. At this stage, we include another specialized component for every stroke, and that is the arrangement.

The Forehand

The player ought to utilize their non-overwhelming hand and keep it on the throat of the racquet as they make their purported unit turn. "Unit turn" implies that the entire body including the arms moves as one unit.

We basically swing to the side while keeping our head confronting forward, and we stretch out both arms to the side. From that point, we discharge the non-prevailing hand, let the racquet drop behind the body and after that draw it forward through the effectively commonplace positions which are the contact point and the complete.

The Two-gave Backhand

We plan in a fundamentally the same as way as we do on the forehand since the stroke is basically a forehand with the non-overwhelming hand. We turn the body to the side while keeping the head confronting forward. While we're turning, we likewise need to modify the grasp of the predominant hand, and we transform it from the eastern forehand grip to the mainland.

We additionally slide the non-prevailing hand starting from the throat to the handle while we're changing the grasp. This fairly complex move must be drilled for some time so it turns out to be snappy and in the long run totally intuitive. From that point, we again let the racquet drop and fall behind us. At that point we pull it through the well known contact point and complete stages that we officially aced.

The One-gave Backhand

We likewise execute the unit turn, however we obviously keep the non-overwhelming hand on the throat of the racquet. We again let the racquet drop, and we discharge the non-predominant hand just before the racquet begins to quicken towards the contact indicate and proceed with the complete.

5. Playing from the Baseline

As you work on hitting from mid-court, you'll soon turn out to be more used to the speed of the ball and the readiness which you included the past stride.

The most ideal approach to add energy to your strokes is to just give your body a chance to locate the most common method for creating more power.

You will actually include a smidgen more body turn and maybe a tiny bit all the more backswing, and the ball will effortlessly achieve your accomplice after one bob.

5 Tennis Tips for Beginners to Accelerate the Learning Curve

While the fundamental stroke strategy is the establishment of figuring out how to play tennis for a total apprentice, there are really different abilities that the play needs to ace with a specific end goal to play tennis well.

The accompanying 5 tips and penetrates for tennis fledglings will help you rapidly defeat the greatest deterrents in taking in tennis without any preparation and permit you to progress rapidly to more elevated amounts.

1. Figuring out how to Judge the Ball

Ball judgment capacity enhances consequently through heaps of playing, yet we can quicken the procedure with one straightforward penetrate.

Basically play the ball after two ricochets rather than one. You'll need to move promote back, obviously, yet you and your accomplice ought to in any case plan to make the main skip in the administration box. This bore will help you perceive how far the ball really pursues the main bob, and that will help you retain its direction.

Play a two-ricochet penetrate for a couple of minutes and afterward do a reversal to playing after one and only skip to check whether your ball judgment capacity has moved forward.

2. The most effective method to Play with "Feel" and Control

A major test for practically every tennis apprentice is that they hit too hard. The moving ball may overpower them and, regardless of the correct stroke movements specified above, despite everything they swing a lot at the ball.

A decent approach to keep that and to figure out how to play tennis with feel is to have the fledgling stand quite recently alongside the net and place the racquet on their accomplice's side.

The accomplice then hurls the ball directly into their racquet, and the amateur needs to play into their hands from that position. The net obviously keeps them from backswing, yet they will acknowledge rapidly that, even with no backswing, they can create enough constrain to make the ball achieve their accomplice.

Following a moment or so playing from this position, move back to the administration line and check whether you can execute this negligible backswing and still play the ball over the net.

3. The most effective method to Play More Relaxed

amateur arcAnother motivation behind why a tennis fledgling can't control the ball well is on account of they are too tight. Maybe despite everything they ponder the guidelines and how to move their arms, or maybe they are influenced by the bobbing ball and basically get to be tense during the time spent hitting it back to their accomplice.

An exceptionally basic however successful method for turning out to be more casual is through getting to be mindful of your strain. The objective is to rate your strain from 1 to 5, 5 being the most tense, 1 being the most casual.

In this way, as you play smaller than usual tennis, ¾ tennis or as of now on the gauge, recall to check with yourself how tense you are from 1 to 5. In the event that you understand that you're at least 3, essentially request that yourself play at level 2 for some time.

You'll see that your body can turn out to be more casual, yet you do need to request that it do that.

4. The most effective method to Play the Ball in an Arc

Tennis apprentices generally believe that a decent shot is the one that goes over near the highest point of the net. That is obviously not valid as that kind of play is exceptionally unsafe.

The most ideal approach to be always reminded that you ought to play in a bend is to utilize a snag at the net. You can put your tennis pack vertically on the seat or put a tennis racquet into the ball bushel or even purchase a more expert instrument like an extraordinary rope that you can extend over the net.

Every one of these hindrances will continually remind you to play in a circular segment and help you instill this thought into your intuitive.

5. The most effective method to Reach the Ball in Time

Amateurs in many cases achieve the ball late and accordingly feel hurried and hit a poor shot. A decent approach to figure out how to take care of business to the ball early is to overstate the circumstance at first.

You can do that by hurrying to the side in the first place, ceasing and sitting tight for your accomplice to sustain you the ball there. This helps you get to be mindful of that space of time between your development and your stroke. What's more, once you're mindful of that brief timeframe, you can now search for it.

In the long run your accomplice sustains the ball to the side first and after that you begin moving towards it, yet now you're mindful that you need to achieve the ball as well as need to achieve the ball with some additional time between your development and your stroke.

Synopsis

The 5 well ordered particular directions for tennis novices and the additional 5 tips for beating the greatest difficulties apprentices face will quicken your learning procedure and help you play and appreciate tennis in a short measure of time.

Taking after these lessons for apprentices will likewise put you in good shape for adapting more propelled tennis aptitudes like adding topspin or cut to your strokes and learning distinctive footwork designs that will rapidly move you from a learner to a middle of the road tennis player and past.

CHAPTER SIX
HOW TO SERVE

Learning how to serve in tennis viably is urgent to your advancement as a player. The following will instruct you concerning how to serve in tennis, beginning with the nuts and bolts.

How to Serve in Tennis is a formative procedure of learning the right tennis serve system

For beginners attempting to see how to serve in tennis, the procedure is usually confusing. It's least demanding in any case the basics of the serve strategy before more advanced ideas can be scholarly.

Tennis Serve Grip
A few players begin with the Eastern forehand hold when first learning how to serve in tennis. To accomplish the Eastern forehand hold, put your hand level on the strings of the racket, and after that move your hand downwards to the handle. Your fingers must be wrapped around the racket. Your first finger ought to be forward marginally.

It's vital that your fingers have no tension — this might be difficult to recollect as you first figure out how to serve in tennis. The eastern forehand hold is regularly called the "shake hands" grasp by the individuals who have quite recently started to figure out how to serve in tennis, on the grounds that, basically, you are shaking hands.

With the Eastern forehand hold, you will probably hit the ball level, that is, without spin; and, not at all like presents with topspin, level serves don't have as much freedom over the net. Therefore, some beginning players can select to utilize the more appropriate serving hold, which is the continental grasp, which naturally gives topspin and sidespin, or cut.

To accomplish the Continental hold, put your palm on the upper right inclination angle — this is 45 degrees counterclockwise from the Eastern forehand grasp. With the Continental hold, the racket face will tilt marginally upward. It is conceivable to hit level with the Continental, yet to do as such you should reach the ball more remote back than common.

While choosing a hold as a learner player, remember that spin is a great deal less vital in the beginning than numerous different elements.

Tennis Serve Motion

At the point when first learning how to serve in tennis, a wind-up is redundant. Attempt a wind-up on the off chance that you wish, in any case; you'll eventually require one — and for a few players, learning how to serve in tennis is less demanding, more agreeable, with a wind-up.

Tennis Serve Toss

Learning how to serve in tennis requires that when you hurl, you imagine a straight line from your starting point to the point where you need to reach the ball; hurl the ball along that line. Keep in mind, likewise, that the higher your hand is the point at which you discharge the tennis ball, the shorter the separation to the point where you'll reach — hence, the ball has less time to stray off base.

You'll need to discharge the ball with as high a scope as could be expected under the circumstances, definitely from at any rate over your head. Discharge all of your fingers from the ball on the double; this, in addition to holding your wrist in a static position, will guarantee the ball remains focused.

Now, we need to focus on your hitting arm. While your using your non-dominant hand to toss up the ball, you're hitting arm ought to swing in reverse to start the striking movement. Also, when you have discharged the tennis ball, start bending your knees and elbow. You will find that you can do your best serve in tennis when you remember to keep your elbow bowed, your wrist loose, and your racket down behind you; these are the key elements that allow you to get the most power with the slightest exertion — and, you won't endure bear injuries, an injury you certainly need to stay away from.

Utilizing the lower body

Make a point to fix your legs, as your approach the contact point. This starts a series of movements that will give the wrist the energy to move upward and forward and give your racket the speed it needs, which conveys energy to the tennis ball.

Here's the way it works: as your legs finish straightening, your elbow ought to rectify also. The power from your legs and parts of your arm is currently exchanged to your wrist, which remains at a ninety-degree edge to your lower arm. All of that power then snaps your wrist forward, this is what creates the speed for your racket. (Another powerful move to the tennis ball originates from turning your body from sideways toward the beginning of the wind-up to facing the net.)

When you are learning how to serve in tennis, you do not need to think about this process — simply keep your racket down, your elbow up, and your arms loose. Keep in mind — don't snap your wrist (a misstep numerous beginners make when learning how to serve in tennis); let it whip forward naturally without any consider exertion on your part, else you'll harm your serve — and perhaps your arm.

Contact Point

Likewise, keep your arm loose and reach up to full expansion; your lower arm will then pronate, the strings facing a great deal more forward. With little exertion, your weight will now exchange forward too, your dominant foot scarcely touching the ground now.

To know how to serve in tennis well, you additionally need to know how to reach the ball in the right spot. To hit a genuinely level serve, you ought to hit the ball at full upwards expansion, roughly ten to twelve inches more remote forward than your head, and ten to twelve inches to the dominant side of your head. You want to try to see your racket make contact with the ball; continue keeping an eye on the contact point for a brief moment a short time later, especially when you're new at learning how to serve in tennis.

Serve Follow through

Once you've made contact with the ball, your dominant foot will probably approach into the court — this is not an issue; you can venture over, or on, the baseline once you've hit the ball. Likewise, as you're learning how to serve in tennis, you may find that during your complete you occasionally hit yourself in the legs with your racket; with practice, you'll figure out how to dependably sidestep your legs on the finish.

You may battle at first as you figure out how to serve in tennis. In any case, it needn't be troublesome on the off chance that you dismember the serve into smaller parts, as we have in the instructions for how to serve in tennis; and ace every segment until you have a respectable serve, tried and true and eventually effective serve; that is, until you've figured out how to serve in tennis.

It takes hone — and, time and persistence — to figure out how to serve in tennis, however once you do figure out how to serve in tennis, you'll appreciate the amusement on a completely new level; and, you'll have a major advantage, dictating points on your administration games. (Advanced players create distinctive serves for various events, however for beginners learning how to serve in tennis, the above tips will serve you well.)

A bore for players learning how to serve in tennis

Finally, here's a practice bore to help you — it's an especially decent bore for when you're at the phase in learning to how to serve in tennis when you're ready to rehearse your point. Go to a vacant court and set up pyramids of ball as an objective; put them near the corners to begin. Work on serving, keeping your point in mind and, as you advance, how much cut you need on your serve.

Rehearse again and again; that is the key. Try different things with wide shots and down the center shots, and with level serves and cut serves. You now know how to serve in tennis with an intention to accomplish more than simply get this show on the road the ball over the net.

CHAPTER SEVEN
HOW TO VOLLEY AND DRILLS FOR IMPROVING YOUR VOLLEY

1. Settle in the "Ready Position"

To assume the ready position make sure the balls of your feet have your weight distributed equally on them and that your legs are shoulder-width apart. You have to remain low with your knees having good flexion and lean marginally forward, ready to respond and detonate similar to a goaltender in a game of hockey. Next, curve your arms and position them before your body. At that point, heads up, a ball is coming at you!

2. Open up your racquet

While planning to reach the ball properly, you need to imagine yourself catching a baseball. Essentially, position the front part of your racquet the way you would a glove, and boom, you've caught the ball!

3. Go ahead, reach

Since you don't need a backswing, you need to utilize the pace of the ball to produce your energy. At that point, essentially edge your racquet fittingly to divert it would where you might want it to go.

4. Practice control over power

Remain certain and leave the steamroller moves for your serve, backhand, and forehand. Placement and control are the keywords in the volley. There's positively no compelling reason to go in swinging and bring your racquet back. It should be like a quick jab not like a right hook. (Left hook for the lefties).

5. Rinse and repeat

Remain light on your feet and perfect, hone, and rehearse! Additionally, to show signs of improvement on your method, concentrate on the total work of your most loved professionals.

Drills

Volley drills are only one part of learning how to play the game. A volley drill acts to build up a player's perseverance, stamina, readiness and sharpness.

Below are a few volley drills that can build up the backhand and forehand volley in tennis.

With good timing and technique, the volley can be carried out without any inconvenience. Having said that, players need to ace the form and should comprehend the best possible timing to carry out the volley.

Serve and Volley drill

In this drill you need to hit a serve, and then an approach volley into the open court. When you serve you must be exceptionally exact as to where you hit the ball. You get two service tries. When you serve for the first time, you have the opportunity to strike the ball with all your force. At the same time be mindful of not making an excessive number of service faults. In this drill, the objective is to get a lot of first serves in. It is also to have the capacity to perform the approach volley to the open court, so that you are set up for a put away volley.

Keep practicing this drill until you can be sure of hitting the ball at the precise spot in the court that you want it to land on. This drill will ensure that you play out the serve and volley effectively in an actual match.

"V" Volley Drill

You do this drill by placing the principal player in the service line (line between the baseline and the net). The other player is in the opposite court and feeds the ball in a manner that the primary player does the V volley drill. You do this volley drill to work on moving advances to the net and simultaneously carry out the volley. As soon as you've returned the ball, instantly come back to your position starting out on the service line. After that the two players need to trade positions. Now the primary player will feed the ball while the other player does the "V" volley drill.

Romanian Volley drill

In this volley drill, players ought to rally to each other exchanging backhand and forehand volleys from the service line. While the players are exchanging volleys, they should rearrange from side-to-side while staying close to the limits of the service boxes. You run this drill from each of the doubles sidelines.

This volley drill is obviously carried out by two players who are situated close to the net. It helps you build up the strength in your forearm so that your racket head remains steady and you have the capacity to return volleys precisely in the net. It isn't easy but if you persevere you'll see that you have improved.

Volley Run drill

The Volley Run drill is drill that can be done by two players. Only the first player has a racket while the second one just tosses the ball at the first player. This drill can be done on both of the most distant side of the court. The second player throws the ball to the main player who volleys it back to the second player.

In the event that the second player gets the ball, the players continue the drill by moving sideways so that the entire net is covered. Once they have covered the entire region of the net (from one end of the net to the other), the players can trade positions. Now the first player feeds the ball to the second player who does the drill.

Cover Volley drill

The best way to do this drill is to involve more than two players. The primary player remains on one side of the court, while the rest of them are situated in the opposite side. The players positioned opposite to the principal player ought to place themselves in a vertical line. Next the ball is aimed by the primary player at the queue's first player's forehand side. Once that player has returned the ball, he or she moves out of the queue and the next in line takes his or her place.

Instead of feeding the ball to the forehand side, the primary player feeds it to the second player's backhand side. Once the second player has hit the ball (or not), he or she moves out and the third player moves up. This goes on until the last player plays out the drill or the player who was first in line can backtrack again and keep the drill going.

Crosscourt and Down the Line Volley drill

The point behind this drill is to improve the stamina, endurance, footwork and anticipation of the ball of the player. For this drill there have to be two players on both sides of the court. The first player needs to hit the ball in a way that it land away from where the second player is standing on the other side of the court. As such, the second player will need to run to be able to return the ball.

Overhead and Volley drill

This drill is crucial if the player wants to become proficient at volleys, footwork and overhead shots. It will likewise assist the player in enhancing his dexterity, speed and reaction quickness. The capacity of the players to respond rapidly to where the ball hits, especially when the adversary hits the ball hard and fast, is known as reaction quickness. The first player stands in the middle of the court while the second player stands in the service box.

Continuous Volley drill

More than two players are needed for this drill. One player stands on one side while the rest stand in two vertical lines on the other side. The single player also known as the feeder, hits the ball at the players in the two lines alternating between backhand and forehand volleys.

Half Court Volley drill

This drill helps you build up your readiness, footwork and speed that ensure that you can volley superbly. It should be done by running to the net as fast as possible.

Volley Drill with left arm at the back

In this drill, you begin by putting your left hand behind your back (in case you are right-handed) and hitting the volley with only your right hand. If you are left-handed you can do this drill with your right hand behind your back while you use your left hand to hit the volley. The drill helps you enhance your focus on the arm with which you hit the ball and your racket head. When your non-dominant hand is behind your back, the hand with the racket is forced to prepare in advance and with no interference from the other hand. It also helps build up the strength in your racket hand so that you can endure the volleys aimed at you that have been hit harder.

CHAPTER EIGHT
HOW TO PLAY THE OVERHEAD

The overhead is not practiced much even though a player can learn the proper technique of the overhead smash through tips.

At the professional level, the overhead smash is a standout amongst the most effortless and capable strokes.

It's a "go to" shot for professionals and is frequently the finishing shot that ends the point and the rival's opportunities to hit any additional shots. Playing these shots is fun but watching them being played is also quite a lot of fun.

The excellence and effortlessness of the overhead smash comes from the imagination of the star players. Combined with awesome physicality, artistic touch and energy, this move is the easiest thing in the world for such players.

Recreational and Club Players' Overheads
The overheads played by recreational players are not so great. The smash isn't a highlight; in fact, they usually tend to stay away from it. The overhead smash is rehearsed once in a while and each player has unrealistic expectations of it. They need to

hit the smash like the geniuses; however without the best possible practice on the right overhead method, hitting a smash like the masters is a one in million shot.

Look at these overhead smash tips to allow your smash to turn into something that you can depend on, instead of hoping that the shot remains in the court.

1. Don't Pray and Spray

The initial overhead smash tip is that you need to have the correct attitude. Having the best possible mindset for the overhead will specifically influence the result. This tip applies to all players.

Most players attempt to hit the smash as hard as they can anyplace they can and implore that it will remain in. Giving little respect to the best possible overhead procedure, they improperly toss their whole body at the ball. They do this without first achieving their balance physically and settling their heads mentally and thinking about a specific area to aim at.

In your head picture and decide where you want to hit the overhead smash, and that will automatically ensure that your body and mind go into the right mode so you can hit it.

2. Quiet your mind

The second tip is to calm your mind when the adversary sends a throw at you. Most players get to be on edge and hurried when the rivals hurl a lob. In the event that you haven't honed the smash in a long while, you might be additionally anxious about making that shot. You may find negative thoughts going through your head before you hit, but if you want to smash effectively your body and mind must be totally centered around simply preparing for the overhead, instead of being distracted by what happened or the result.

3. Overhead smash requires fast footwork

Another basic misinterpretation and conviction among recreational players with regards to the overhead is that it needs next to no footwork. This overhead smash tip applies to all those players who have block feet with regards to the smash. Most players dawdle when they observe that overhead smash coming, as opposed to rapidly moving in reverse and getting into the right position with fast initial body planning.

A key overhead smash tip is to recollect is to prepare for the overhead at the earliest opportunity, directly after acknowledgment of the rival's initial shot. Try not to hold up too long to get your feet started. You might be tempted to hold up or move gradually with the ball speed, yet this will just make you late for the overhead resulting in a pitiable and frail smash.

4. **Quick readiness**

An essential tip for the overhead smash is to start the preparedness and begin moving in reverse at the earliest opportunity. This also means the footwork, and in particular the abdominal area. While moving in reverse, make a point to bring the hand with the racket up in the power position and abstain from taking an intemperate backswing. The abdominal area will be loaded if you've done a compact prep and help with the coil when preparing.

5. **Keep the left arm up**

A decent overhead smash tip is to keep non-dominant hand up throughout your motion to the overhead. Star players can keep the non-dominant hand up during the whole smash. Keeping the left arm up helps in tracking the ball and maintaining the best possible position for the shoulder. It likewise maintains the correct curl which will help with generating power.

Try not to point at the ball when you're hitting the overhead. All you need to do is to keep your left arm pointed at the sky during the whole stroke. It will encourage a characteristic, proficient and easy tennis overhead smash.

6. **Don't retreat to the overhead smash**

It's tempting to surge the overhead and get there as quickly as time permits. The body's initial inclination is to retreat with a specific end goal to move in reverse. This will mislead your adjust totally, and actually ensure that you are slower to touch base to the overhead smash. Instead, you have to move in reverse using jumble steps or cross strides which will kick off much speedier footwork. Consider this the most vital overhead smash tip of them all.

The footwork utilized as a part of the tennis smash is like that of some different instances in different games. In football, football player must discover the football using three stage drops, five stage drops and even seven stage drops. What they comprise of is fast, small and dangerous hybrid or crossback steps, and these means are fast fire and rapidly recover the player and ready to get the ball. This is particularly the same for the tennis overhead. Instead of using retreat steps and potentially tripping and falling, remain in great adjust using crossback or rearrange steps.

7. Get and Stay Sideways Through the Hit

This overhead smash tip can have a major effect on your capacity to create a power overhead smash versus a frail dinker. When you perceive that your adversary is sending you a smash, turn sideways immediately – and from that point begin moving in reverse using either crossover steps or shuffle steps. Ensure your feet are spread at least shoulder-width in distance or more prominent as you move into position to hit the overhead smash. I get a kick out of the chance to position the feet no less than two shoulder widths apart, while keeping a solid athletic establishment. This keeps my center of gravity low and ensures that I stay low while hitting the overhead.

8. Use the whole body to hit the smash

The smash is not a shot that comes from your entire arm, keeping in mind most of the power as it appears will comprise of having a decent arm movement recollect that with a specific end goal to create an effective overhead smash you have to utilize your entire body.

Don't ever stand totally upright when you are in the process of moving or hitting the overhead. Instead, make it a point to remain low and make snappy small strides when you are moving to hit the overhead.

9. Don't Be A Sitting Duck

It's tempting to stay where you are and observe the overhead smash go through the air, and it might be hard to figure out the exact flight trajectory of the ball coming in at you. It might appear to be anything but difficult to just rise up with your arm as opposed to assuming the right and correct position to hit every single time. However, when you force your body to make the additional strides necessary to smooth out your balance, it will mean the difference between a a poor shot and a respectable overhead smash.

10. Develop a Fluid and Smooth Arm Action

The overhead smash method is a crucial part of a decent smash. Figure out how to build up a smooth arm motion so that you can hit the overhead smash. Abstain from taking an inordinate backswing or hazard hitting late. The overhead is an intense stroke when implemented accurately and with the best possible arm motion.

These tips for the overhead smash are intended to instruct players to take in the smash and dispose of the most well-known missteps made on the overhead. Another imperative part of the tennis overhead smash is the system.

Rehearse these overhead smash tips as much as possible and with the best possible measure of practice time you can claim the overhead smash shot in a matter of moments.

CHAPTER NINE
WHAT BEGINNERS NEED TO KNOW

The easiest way to talk about tennis and its related strategies is to first consider the aim of the tennis player, both from an objective point of view as a game (how to score points, how to win, how to outwit your opponent) and from a personal point of view in terms of how an individual wants to improve as a player.

For beginners, the general rule is often 'aim down the middle and deep.' Essentially this serves two functions: first, for those who haven't honed their swing yet, it's easier to aim down the middle in order to ensure that you get the ball onto the other side of the court, and second the way the net is hung means that it is generally lower in the center than it is on the sides, even when it's been tightened up. This serves a good foundational strategy from whence a player can then interpret his opponent based on five primary actions:

1. From the baseline, many players try to aim to an opponent's left. This is a vital trick since most players will be right-handed, meaning that the racket will be

on their right side – this immediately makes their left side vulnerable, except to a backswing.

2. It is also possible to aim to an opponent's right. While this may seem redundant since you are hitting *toward* their racket, used in conjunction with other swings, it can prove to be just as effectual if the timing is right.

3. Over their head: this one involves the ball flying over an opponent's head, and should only be attempted if a.) they're the sort of opponent that tries to hit every ball or b.) they're very close to the net and you can lift the ball over their head but still keep it in bounds.

4. Most players learn quickly to aim for an opponent's feet. This maximizes your chance of keeping the ball on the court while still forcing your opponent to 'reach' for it, often opening up a gap for you to exploit when they return the ball.

5. Pushing the ball *through* an opponent is also an excellent tactic, involving a very hard fast swing that will take them by surprise and prevent them from attacking the net.

The goal of each of these actions, used individually or in tangent with one another to create a system of hits, is to make your opponent *move*. We'll go into more depth about the psychology and mental strategies involved in upping your game in a later chapter, but for now let's take a look at the physical elements of tennis.

Serving And Returning – Tips

There are numerous methods for serving and receiving the ball, but the general practice is to try and get a good rally going (i.e.,. the back and forth between two players). Serving is split into overhand or underhand serves, but are all classified according to four main serves, which all have their advantages and disadvantages.

- The flat serve laterally crosses the net and is easy to learn, while its speed helps confuse opponents and conserves your energy.

    o These generally have no spin, and their main aim is to simply get the ball over the net. Hit in the center of your racket.

- The slice serve is also easy to learn and involves the wall hitting and veering away from a player, giving the opponent even less time to react, though its commonness makes it easy to return.

    o When hitting a slice serve, it's important to *lightly* brush the ball off-center of the racket, usually to the right – one mistake that's easy to make is not continuing to carry through with the stroke.

- The kick-serve is harder to learn and involves the ball hitting and bouncing high or toward an opponent, making it harder to attack and is a useful serve against beginners who may be unfamiliar with this style.
  - In order to pull off a kick-serve we again brush the ball, left to right, but maintain a low to high angle of around 8 o'clock to 2 o'clock.
- The top-spin serve is also easy to learn, but by giving the ball an edge it tends to be faster than the flat serve, bounces high because of its spin, and is still hard to attack.
  - The top-spin is similar to the kick-serve, but the angle is a bit more acute, around 6 o'clock to 1 o'clock – the speed and parabola of the spin will be determinate on how hard you hit the ball.

While each serve can be used to a different effect, most of us default to one or two. Learning how to capitalize on the strengths and weaknesses of each is imperative in the long-game, especially against opponents who will be learning and adapting to your hits. There are a few other tricks and techniques we'd like to focus on (as well as a few no-no's that even the professionals make) that can be considered while serving. These include:

- Keeping a consistent and fast pace with your racket head – often the effectiveness of a serve has more to do with speed than mechanics. If you find that you are not consistently able to hit the backstop with a serve, <u>try pronating your arm several degrees</u>.

- Make sure your toss is consistent - if you find there is some variability in how far your serves reach, it again may have nothing to do with your actual serve but with an inconsistent toss that forces you to compensate each time.

- Know which stance works for you: there are two stances in tennis, pinpoint and platform, and each has its own advantages and disadvantages.

    o Pinpoint Stance: involves both feet close to one another, and usually results in a faster serve because you are able to jump a little higher. The downside is that you may have less control over the ball and your balance is naturally compromised by having your feet so close together.

- Platform Stance: obviously the biggest advantage is more balance since it involves a wider stance – a shoulder's width apart – and is a good way to get a consistent serve going; plus, you never have to worry about foot-faulting.

While serving has its own system of rules and technique, *returning* is just as important. The main goal of the return is to get a rally going by <u>keeping the ball in play</u> – keeping this in mind while initiating one of the several strokes is one of the most fundamental skills for a successful game.

- Forehand – for the forehand return, always remember to keep the racket in front of you until you're ready to hit the ball; many players, including professionals, sometimes get a little too casual and allow their racket to fall – *keeping the racket in front of your face limits delay in reaction time and prompts a quick response!*
  - The proper angle and distance of the backhand, as you bring the racket into position, varies depending on teacher and personal style, but in general make sure you're not "over backhanding" – many people are worried about not getting enough momentum, and pull far back on their backhand, but this can

lead to a bad habit that will affect the timing of your swings.

- o Make sure when you hit the ball the racket is to your side and *in front* of you – again, waiting until the ball is parallel to your body is an easy habit to get into, and seriously reduces reaction time and control.

- o Lastly, also carry through with your footwork; this means adjusting your weight to your left foot when you swing and lifting your right heel.

- Backhand – for both double and single-handed backhands, we often see problems arising from too rigid a stance. The shoulders should be allowed to rotate so that they're 90 degrees to the body.

  - o With backhands, the footwork is often reversed, so make sure you're pushing off the left foot and putting your weight on the right. This will help with a fluid movement of the body and allow it to recoil back to a ready position.

  - o This technique of letting the body do the work by having the coil and rotation of the shoulders give the power means the racket is simply carried along and eliminates the work of the arms (and is another good way to conserve energy and avoid injury).

- Don't forget to extend! This is something even the professionals often overlook; regardless of how powerful your backhand might be, without a good extension you'll limit yourself severely as to the types of returns you can make – extending the arm outward as part of the carry-through ensures you greater control over the ball in terms of adding spin and direction.

CHAPTER TEN
SOME EXERCISES FOR BEGINNERS

A well-known axiom goes, "with new levels, there's new Devils", and the devoted tennis player is going to encounter this saying at some point of time. A player can rehearse heaps of aptitude work and achieve a specific level, however this "new devil" sneaks around, stopping the player from attaining the uppermost level that he or she can.

This "new devil" is basically nothing but the lack of fitness or strength, or worse yet, both. The higher you go in tennis, the more important these two factors become. Indeed, even the well-known Roger Federer exposed that he performs at least one hundred hours of conditioning and strength throughout the off-season.

It is beyond uncertainty that strength training is available in numerous structures and molds. There are bands, balls, boxes, bars, chimes, plates, and various machines. It is not possible to discuss all of them in detail here, yet I would say, I have utilized, tried and explored different avenues regarding numerous types of preparation. The rundown underneath includes those exercises that I observed to be straightforward and simple to actualize, especially when it comes to the novice.

It is difficult to uncover the best strength activities for a player without being able to understand that the most excellent activities are normally ones that require a great deal of method work. Despite the fact that I support doing front squats, back squats and numerous varieties of lifts meant for the Olympics, I comprehend that the lifts can just profit those players that can legitimately learn them. Else, they can cause more damage than great without appropriate coaching and supervision. As such, I am not including the most advanced activities. Likewise, a large number of players may not be exceptionally experienced when it comes to weights so one rundown would not be enough and numerous great ones may be forgotten.

All things considered, the rundown beneath is just a START; the list is meant for the novice and needs practically zero weight room encounter. This chapter just manages the novice list in the first place. Once you are proficient at these, you can go for intermediate and then advanced exercises.

Single Leg Press

In many gyms you will come across a large number of equipment. The leg press is one such machine and gives the beginner an extraordinary leg workout with no reason for them having to take in a bundle of method. Strength in the legs is fundamental in this game. A player needs to increase their strength most especially in the legs so that they can move all the more effectively for longer timeframes. Likewise, single appendage work is critical for tennis since tennis players quite often are imbalanced from their non-racket to their racket side. This exercise deals directly with this issue. The practice permits you to create leg strength with no going in favor of your racket side.

Essentially, you need to keep one leg on the stage, where you feel most agreeable, then discharge the weight and start. As you push the weight downwards, make certain to not give your knee a chance to twist internally, instead ensure that your knee remains straightforwardly at the level of the ball of the foot. While descending you need to try not to permit your knee to move past your toes. To finish, you need to get the weight downwards until the knee is bent at ninety degrees, and then shove the weight into a practically bolted out arrangement.

Move on into the following repetition without any delay or stopping. Begin with a light weight, force out about eight to ten repetitions. You need to keep adding weights in every set. Do this until you complete 4 sets. The final set ought to be extreme and coming near disappointment.

Abduction

This is another mechanism that enhances the strength in the player's hips. The abductors in the glutes and hips are in charge of improving the balance, soundness, and the strength of sideways motion that becomes so essential in the game.

Technically, the competitor sits in the abduction apparatus and the legs are secured alongside the resistance arms. At this point, the competitor needs to push their legs in opposition to the pads in an outward direction. This is done until the legs are positioned wide and far separated as could be expected under the circumstances. At that point, the athlete moves the legs together, and then rehashes the motion. Try not to jolt the weight or loosen during the motion at all. Try to remain in control. You will be able to feel the working of the hip abductor muscles.

You need to do 15 reps in one set and do three sets, ensuring that the last one is as tough as possible.

Adduction

This exercise and the machine for this exercise are the opposite of what I discussed above. At some point, the player finds himself or herself going sideways. The job of adductors is to balance out the leg before the player makes strikes. The muscles in the groin are called adductors and are not trained very well. As such, weariness and the possibility of injury are high.

In this case, the competitor needs to sit in the adduction device. The legs are secured alongside the resistance arms. At this point, the competitor needs to push the legs towards each other in opposition to the pads. Do this until the legs are as one and after that, while still under control, permit the legs to be separated as far as possible under the circumstances, and then repeat the motion. Try not to yank the weight or loosen up during the motion at all. Remain in control. You will be able to feel the working of the hip adductor muscles (the groin).

You need to do 15 reps in one set and do two sets, ensuring that the last one is as tough as possible

Hyperextension

The glutes and lower back muscles are important stabilizers of the torso or "core". This exercise works the glutes, hamstring and back erector muscles. All these muscles are vital for players who are rushing to hit a shot at the net or to a drop shot. These muscles are the accelerator and sprint muscles for the player.

The athlete needs to put their legs beneath the ankle pads and position the quads alongside the upper pads. Fold the arms over the mid-section or behind the head. The body needs to be facing in the direction of the ground and outward throughout the motion. Fix the entire body. Don't forget the legs. Starting here, you need to lower the abdominal area in the direction of the ground. Do this until the middle is at around a 45-degree point. This will ensure steady and predictable strain in all the needed muscle bunches. From here, amplify body until it is in a straight line, while squeezing the hamstrings and glutes at the highest point of the rep. Every rep ought to be controlled, particularly in transit down, then speedier going up.

Begin with a light weight. Drive out around 10-12 reps. Keep adding weight every set until four sets are complete. The final set ought to be intense and coming near disappointment.

1-DB Upright Row

The vast majority of the abdominal area movements that players make are focused on the anterior region, meaning that aptitudes like forehand and serving works principally on the "front" of your body. Since these aptitudes are concentrated on a single side. As such, using 1-DB Upright Rows, the idea is to adjust strength levels from one part of the shoulders to the other.

Basically the competitor will get one DB; he or she will then let it suspend at the focal point of the body at abdomen tallness. From that point, he or she will lift the DB, pushing the elbow up and out. Keep doing this until the DB is right below the armpit. Repeat the motion, while keeping it under control. You will feel the muscles work on the side of the shoulder and upper back.

Do 15 reps and 3 sets of those reps. Start light and add weights every set, ensuring that the final set is as troublesome as could reasonably be expected without loss of technique.

DB High Incline Press

Because of the amount of work that is done by the foremost side of the abdominal area, we should set it up, work on it, and reinforce it so that it can withstand better the amount of training and matches. As such, DB Incline Press can be an awesome practice to strengthen the upper mid-section and front of the shoulders.

Basically increase the edge of a seat. Get two DBs. Lift the DBs to the highest point of your shoulders and squeeze them overhead. Bring them down to the highest point near the shoulders. Rehash the press. Don't lock your elbows at the top of the movement; the pressure must be on the shoulders during motion.

Do 12 reps and 3 sets, begin genuinely light, and afterward advance up in weights every set making final set troublesome and close to disappointment.

Seated Rows

This practice is done on an appliance. There is support for your abdominal area regardless of it being a leverage or cable machine. This practice is an incredible postural practice that works opposing muscle bunches that are required to play tennis. Most shoulders, upper and lower back pain occurs because of absence of support provided by your posture. The seated rows exercise reinforces the upper back in order to provide the player a greatly improved base from which to carry out serves, backhands and forehands with better steadiness.

Technically, the competitor sits on the seat, solidly puts their mid-section alongside the pad (you can correct the pad to an agreeable tallness), and after that gets the handles. Then he or she pulls the handles toward them. As the weight comes nearer, drive your mid-section up, bending the muscles of the upper back. Gradually move the weight to initial position, and afterward rehash the rep.

You need to do eight to ten reps and four sets. Add a weight every set and attempt two troublesome sets.

Weighted Crunches

Obviously, our rundown would require an abdominal practice to complete it. Starting with basic crunches is the most ideal approach, especially when there is resistance. Ordinarily we deal with abdominal muscles uniquely in contrast to other muscle bunches. We train different muscles using resistance, go with heavy weights, and are dynamic in the training arrangements, yet when it comes to abs, we need to stay with high reps, add no weights, and our arrangements do not have any sort of progress when it comes to strength.

With our arrangement here, we need to load the motion, yet keep great technique. As such, you need to rest with your back level to the floor. Snatch a 5 or 10 lb plate and expand your arms straight until the weight is straight over your face. Next lift your feet so your knees are at a 90-degree point to your body. Keep your chin off your mid-section at all times. Finally, flex your abs, comfortable gut catch while driving the weight toward the ceiling. Ensure you are using your abdominal muscles as it were. The development is a sum of roughly 4 inches.

Do 3 sets of 15 redundancies.

Exercise center Routine Wrap Up

Tennis is a hazardous game, yet one that is extremely tedious and goes on for a considerable length of time at once. Better strength levels are critical to make a higher potential for touchiness and additionally building a superior establishment for development proficiency and overall conditioning.

In the event that a player isn't sufficiently solid, his or her development turns out to be less proficient and accordingly assesses the body substantially more. Making the player substantially more drained!

With respect to our rundown... There are varieties of all of these lifts, all of which are exceptionally viable. You can utilize different groups, selectorized machines, and barbells and execute comparative developments. In any case, the key is to begin some place and build up some consistency and this rundown is an extraordinary begin.

The activities are simple technically, extremely central, and sufficiently fundamental to increase sufficiently strength to advance to the following level of strength training. Following a month or so of using this rundown, then we can proceed onward to an intermediate arrangement. Stay tuned. Glad Training.

CHAPTER ELEVEN
ADVANCED STRATEGIES

You'll learn tennis system and tennis strategies right here. In the event that you integrate them into how you play your game, you'll find that you're a more capable competitor on the tennis court.

Need to take in somewhere in the range of tennis technique to improve your qualities and adventure your adversaries' shortcomings? Need to take in about tennis strategies to accomplish your tennis methodologies? Read on!

The most excellent players don't just have incredible techniques, they ace stratagem with advanced strategic arrangements. Their tennis procedure and strategies permit them to manage any circumstance and adapt their style of playing so they are effective.

What do players with superior tennis procedure and tennis strategies know?
Firstly, they know what their style, qualities and shortcomings are, and how to utilize all of these in the most efficient manner possible. This means that, bosses of tennis systems and tennis strategies know their amusement and how they can force it on

their rivals. Furthermore, by scrutinizing their rival for the duration of warm-up, they rapidly get to be mindful of how their opponent plays, and his or her techniques.

Sophisticated tennis players search for shortcomings in their rival's method, development, weight exchange, and response time. Players who have advanced tennis techniques and tennis strategies watch the shots their adversary lean towards. Furthermore, those with superior tennis techniques and tennis strategies rapidly understand the mental attributes of their rival. Is he or she excessively fearless and self-assured or indecisive and missing certainty, and whatnot?

The information above is gathered throughout warm-up as well as the initial couple of minutes of playing, and a strategic arrangement for making more highly developed tennis systems is framed; considerably new information is accumulated all through the game, and the strategies for moving forward tennis methodologies are polished.

Win More Points

The most excellent tennis procedures are like those in any game: win additional points; let go of fewer points. However, what tennis strategies bolster a tennis methodology of more points being won? Utilize the learning you've got by scrutinizing your rival. For instance, you've watched what your rival's weaker side is. Then assault this weaker agree with groundstrokes, serves and returns. Constrain your adversary to utilize this weaker side; play speedier shots to that part, so that your rival has less time to respond. Utilize varieties of tallness, speed and spin to upset your rival's timing.

Watching for Weaknesses is Vital

In the event that your rival is tall, make sure that the ball lands low, which will force him or her to twist. In the event that your rival shows up unfit or moderate, drive him or her to keep running from one side to the other or from deep to shallow and then back. A complete exhibit of strategies can be connected to most amusement circumstances, permitting you to play better than your adversary, in this manner getting more points. Maybe, for instance, amongst all your strategies you may have one that dictates that you play more aggressively and do so from the baseline.

Conflicting strategies might be utilized to accomplish this optional procedure: you may hit balls on the ascent to put weight on your rival; or you may employ whatever number of back to front forehands as could be expected under the circumstances. On the other hand, if for instance, your adversary is not comfortable at the net, you can play short and then lob or you can force your rival to volley.

Keep in mind to remain adaptable and strong all through your match; if a stroke does not work out, don't persistently continue trying to play it to bolster your tennis systems despite the fact that it's clearly "off". What's more, in opposition to all of your rivals, it's vital to mask your strokes and shift your situations; trickery is imperative to your tennis procedures, more vital even — on occasion — than pure power or system is to sustaining your tennis strategy.

Make Fewer Errors

Furthermore, what tennis strategies bolster tennis strategies of losing less points? Keep in mind, your rival is trying to do the same to you also; that is part of his or her tennis system. As such you have to be able to counteract the attacking game he or she is playing. You'll consequently lose less points while gaining more since — dissimilar to games such as basketball or soccer — the scoring in tennis dependably gives somebody a point.

First of all, dependably utilize your qualities until your rival constrains you into doing something else. Yet, suppose your rival — to bolster his or her procedures — is taxing your less strong side; how would you kill this assault? Utilize your shot that is weaker to remain in the rally. You need to remember that your tennis system and tennis strategies here are not to win more points, but rather to lose less points.

At that point, once losing less points, you utilize intelligent strategies to gain more points, one of your two tennis methodologies. Attempt to utilize your weaker shot to confront your rival's weaker side — then end the point with a solid shot, likely a volley or forehand approach shot. Do this by means of your weaker shot to make your adversary stay far away from the baseline and sidelines; make him or her move to the net and hurl, or force him or her to play a volley on his or her weaker side. Doing this will hold back your rival's tennis methodology.

Add Variety

You can likewise astonish your rival with a drop shot or moon ball. At that point, when you've set up a small, frail ball, assault your rival with your solid shot. Try not to go out on a limb along these lines making superfluous blunders and letting go a point — it does not bolster your tennis procedure; play to remain in the point until you get the chance to win a point. The individuals who are not so keen with their techniques and strategies regularly attempt to hit hostile shots in order to win a point from places where they ought to attempt to hit cautious shots so as to lose less points.

Your adversary may likewise serve to the side that is weaker for you — to bolster his or her techniques, forcing botches or powerless returns. What strategies bolster your techniques of losing less points now? You need to move back beyond what many would consider possible, giving yourself an opportunity to determine the ball and reach. Continue defending with changed shots — whether they are low cuts, moon balls or moderate balls — determining what kills your adversary's swing.

Responding to the Opponent's Shot

Presently suppose your rival is using varieties of speed, spin or tallness to disturb your timing. How would you kill this assault? You need to remember that your strategies are not meant to win more points, but rather to lose less points. Understand the ball. The individuals who are bosses at tennis methodologies and tennis strategies do well at this, watching shots precisely, rapidly reading the tallness, spin, and direction.

It's additionally essential to recognize what is your most excellent profit for different shots. Here again, those who have advanced tennis techniques and tennis strategies know the way they play their games. They know what their qualities are and best they can be used. Frequently, on the off chance that you get a low cut, you need to give back a low cut, and if you get a high ball, you need to give the same back.

Furthermore, if your rival volleys and serves on first serves — another strategy to bolster his or her technique; how would you kill this assault? You have to compel a confounded volley. You can either move back, giving you enough time for a compelling swing that profits a fastball; or you can move inside the court, thereby blocking the ball and making it land at your rival's feet; or discern your adversary's volley that is weaker and try to make the ball land on that side.

Everything above kills your adversary's game; these are not hostile tennis strategies, but instead those of losing less points. Of course, you need to know how you can win more points and how you can lose less points; remember both as you examine your adversary's and your qualities and shortcomings.

CHAPTER TWELVE
SINGLE PLAYER STRATEGIES

The single player game is perhaps one of the most important in tennis, whether you're playing with friends at a pick-up game or deep in a tournament cycle. In general, we talk about the single player strategy as being comprised of both a short and long game – this corresponds to how you immediately respond to any given situation (whether it be a return or a starting serve) in the heat of the moment, and your long-term strategy of how you plan to outwit/outpace your opponent.

In general every player will naturally find his or her own particular strengths and weaknesses and work toward towards them – in this chapter we look at some of the more common tips that keep in mind and also look at how individual styles can affect performance by analyzing a few tennis legends.

First and foremost, we come back to that old proverbial imperative: "keep the ball deep and down the middle". For single players, where you find yourself during a game can make or break whether or not you win.

- Positioning – the key to 'controlling the court' comes down to a number of variables, but your positioning on the court is a big one. By staying to the center of the court, you're giving yourself the maximum amount of movement and using the space to your advantage; often times beginner players tend to deviate over time, favoring either the left or right-hand side of the court – <u>always check yourself after each attack to make sure you're back at center</u>!

- Related to positioning is your movement laterally up and down the court – most teachers and trainers try to emphasize a steady movement *forward* as opposed to backward. This serves two functions: first, we are creatures of body language, and moving forward instinctively forces an opponent back, shortening their range and movement on the court. Second, it helps you maintain control of the court.

- Be relentless! This might seem obvious, but it's easy to get stuck in a back and forth rally that doesn't go anywhere. Always forcing the attack at every opportunity, <u>especially</u> as a first return from an opponent's serve, gives you an immediate edge.

- Betting on the odds – even after an hour of playing for the first time in their life, a beginner will reflexively be able to tell you where their strengths and weaknesses are in terms of returns, serving, footwork, and overall technique. What distinguishes the expert from the rookie is that the expert can work these percentages to their favor; it may sound a bit less than proactive, but sticking with what works and maintaining a consistency during a game is often the best approach. Alternatively, use your practice time on your own to master new shots or serves.

Rhythm

The more you play and the longer you develop your tennis skills, the more you'll hear the word 'rhythm' thrown around – "I really found my rhythm today" or "He lost his rhythm in that last set". To talk about rhythm is to describe something that avoids empirical definition. It's the same sort of thing that athletes refer to when they talk about 'being in the zone' or 'having *it*'.

Essentially, rhythm comes down to a synthesis of different skillsets aligning and resulting in a balance between all aspects of your game. But again, we can't stress the importance of consistency enough – when all of your serves, returns, and general playing style come together, you've managed to find your rhythm.

And just as every person is unique, so too is every person's rhythm. Some might find that they are able to get into a perfect psychological and physical synchronization quite easily, while for others it might take time to warm up. Regardless, being able to recognize when you're in your rhythm is as crucial as being able to pick up on *your opponent's* rhythm. We'll take a closer look at the psychological implications of tennis later, but there are a few techniques we can apply here in terms of technique:

- Breaking Rhythm – for the single player, learning how to both maintain their own rhythm while disrupting your opponent's is basic Tennis 101. There are a number of ways to break your opponent's rhythm.

    o First and foremost, don't fall into a <u>static game</u>. As we've seen, making your opponent move helps to separate intermediate players from beginners. Don't rely on the same attacks, and vary your approach by hitting both high/low and left/right. This prevents your opponent from adapting and keeps him or her on their toes.

    o Second, know what we mean when we say "overplay" – often an opponent will have a weaker side, and centering your shots here will force him to overplay, often taking him off balance. Conversely, this will also decrease the amount of time an opponent is able to use his strengths. For example, forcing backhand attacks from an opponent in order to reduce the number of times he is able to use a more powerful forehand return.

- o Thirdly, try to get in as many cross-court diagonal shots as possible; we've seen that the center of the net is lower than the sides so this adds to the percentage of being able to win a given attack; the diagonal shots, especially if <u>they're high bounces</u>, are difficult to return.

The Long Game

A lot of the tips above are great in the short term, especially as reactions to surprise serves by an opponent or a way to keep yourself in the game, but when you're playing against a determined opponent for an extended period of time, you need a plan.

Essentially, you'll either fall into three categories: defensive, offensive, or mixed. A defensive player will do anything to stay in the game, and there is a great deal of endurance and stamina required. On the other hand an offensive player may try to end the game as quickly and efficiently as possible with well-timed attacks and powerful hits, and wear herself out quickly. Obviously, then, there is something to be said for a mixed player who is able to accommodate a blend of both of these spectrums.

There are no hard and straight rules about how to organize your long game strategy, but there are definitely common variables: a.) figuring out where your opponent is weakest and pushing this weakness until you score a point and/or wear her down, b.) relying on your own strengths and trying to anticipate your opponent's behavior, and c.) being adaptable to the game as it progresses, and not being squeamish about changing things up halfway through – <u>what works well in the beginning of the game may not work very well, or at all, by the end of the game!</u>

CHAPTER THIRTEEN
DOUBLE PLAYER STRATEGIES

A lot of times you might find yourself teaming up with another player, especially if you're playing tennis more for fun than in a tournament or professional format. With four people on the court now, the sorts of strategies and techniques that might've won you a set in a singles only game don't necessarily apply here. The entire dynamic of a double player involves, above all else, a degree of *cooperation* that isn't present in other styles.

This highlights our first strategy, and one that is obvious on the face:

- Choosing The Right Partner – generally speaking, if you're playing doubles it means that you probably know your partner and have developed a rapport of sorts. This will be crucial in creating a relationship that is mutually symbiotic and a boon to both players and the game.
    - Know Each Other's Weaknesses – just as it is important in singles games to know your own weakness, it's *vital* to let your partner know in a

doubles game; this will help them pick up the slack. For example, if you have a weak game when it comes to getting wide shots, they might be able to cover more of the court and let you handle side shots.

- Leader vs. Follower – it's just part of being human, but we are naturally leaders or followers, and in tennis this actually works well. If you're more comfortable picking up the slack, or if they're more assertive at getting the ball, you'll have an overall more well-rounded collective skillset; a lot of doubles matches falter because both players are either docile, and won't take the initiative, or both are too assertive and end up battling for each ball.

- Rely On The 'I' Formation – if one of you is comparatively weaker as a server, or your opponents' return is extremely strong, this tactical formation can really confuse opponents; the partner of the server squats down near the net while the server hits the ball just behind them.

In a doubles game there are also a few mistakes that singles only players often make. Because there are double the amount of people on the court, the singles approach of trying to make every ball count doesn't work quite as well – you'll practically exhaust yourself trying to make *every* attack a winning one. With double players, it's important to trust your teammate and <u>exercise patience in waiting for the right time</u> to strike.

The back and forth volleying in a doubles game is also more intensive; don't fight it. Instead, use the opportunity of a longer back-and-forth interaction to gauge your opponents' opening – this will eliminate the number of 'free points' accrued through careless errors on your part and increase the chance of scoring on them.

Three Big Serving Tips:

- In a doubles game, the <u>fast serve doesn't always work out</u>. Both sides of an opponent's court are covered, so even if you put a comet tail on the ball, chances are it's being covered – additionally, a big swing will reduce the amount of time you have to recover from an opponent's return.

- Avoid flat serves – for the same reasons as above, a flat serve is easy to return in a doubles game because both sides of the court are occupied. Instead, focus on your slices and top-spin serves; these will give you more of an opening to return a volley and will force the opposition to move, possibly weakening their formation (and giving *your* teammate the chance to exploit a gap and poach a good shot).

- Avoid top-spin ground strokes – this one is a bit of a doozy, since a low flying top-spin is a good thing in a singles game. In a doubles game its weakness is self-apparent: to get a good top-spin ground stroke you would have to hit the ball from far back on your court, and the long winding shot is easy prey on a doubles' court. The one exception to this is if you can consistently put a low angle spin on the ball, knocking it at your opponent's feet (otherwise you're just giving the shot away).

Another few big no-no's in doubles tennis center around (again) techniques that are beneficial in singles games. These include, most famously, the smash shot. When you've gotten close to the net and want to try and make a winning attack, a lot of people in doubles tennis go in for the hard smash shot – while this may pay off once in a while, it also puts you at an immediate disadvantage if the opponent returns, especially <u>with a lob shot over your head</u>. Opponents who are good at returning smashes also realize that a.) they don't have to work very hard to return the ball and lob it over your head, and therefore it's a good way to exhaust you and b.) you'll probably try to hit the ball harder and put more speed on it, but to no avail.

If you *are* set on these sorts of attacks, then it's crucial to work out a system with your partner so that they can cover you in case of such a return. And, according to the age old truism: down the middle and deep. This is especially true in doubles tennis because putting it down the middle forces confusion among your opponents as to who will return any given attack.

The First Serve

Again and again in doubles strategy you'll also hear that the first serve is the most important. This is for some reasons, most prominently that the first serve (either on your end of the court or your opponents') will usually set the tone of the rest of the game. If your first serve misses or fails, this will bolster your opponent's next hit, and could also cause tension between you and your teammate.

- That said, there are a few things to consider: first, it is better to set a safe game than to overplay and miss the net. If you're not as confident with your serves, this is not the time to be trying out a new kind of serve or technique – play it safe and get the ball over the net, then deal with the volley to further set the tone of the game between you and your partner.

- Because in a doubles match it is vital to aim for your opponent's feet, consider using a slice serve or a kick serve than a normal flat serve. This will give to your percentage during the first volley, and also throw off your opponent's game.

- Placement Over Power – this again comes down to the fact that entire court is now being occupied; adding more power to shots will only exhaust you, increase the likelihood of injury, and often give your opponent the chance to work on *his* placement.

Communication

A no-brainer, really, but because it seems like such an obvious element of the doubles game, this is precisely why good communication is often overlooked even by the professionals who might just assume it or take it for granted. Being able to effectively communicate with your partner *will* determine how well the two of you cooperate and whether or not you win or lose a game.

Verbalize – there is a lot to be said for body language, and there is definitely a 'cool' factor when you're able to indicate a plan of attack to your partner with nothing more than a gesture or a look; but don't let pride ruin your game, and don't assume that you're being understood. Verbalizing and talking to your teammate after every serve or return will get you both in the habit of talking to one another and you'll immediately find that you're able to work more cooperatively by being better able to anticipate the other's reaction. Verbalizing also increases morale, and keeps the game light and amicable, while still maintaining a sense of competition.

Cover The Middle – depending on how circumstances unfold, a lot of the time you or your partner will have to move left or right depending on the return from an opponent. When this happens, the middle of the court becomes a gap. This vulnerability is a very attractive target to opponents, so being able to anticipate your partner's movement and move inward to cover the middle is probably the most important thing you can do. A lot of training manuals refer to the analogy of windshield wipers and being able to synchronize your movements (perpendicularly and laterally) with your partner to cover as much of the court as possible.

Figure Out Cues – especially useful during serves, having some special gestures or cues can also really give you and your partner an edge. Some might include a fist or open hand to indicate that your partner should "Stay" or "Poach", but professionals take it even further and develop a system for telling their partner what they'll do *after* the serve – i.e. move left or right.

Poach/Stay Switch – the poach versus stay approach to a game is a staple of doubles tennis and involves the serving player immediately covering the opposite side of the court so that the net player can poach; however one huge mistake even professionals make is <u>to stay even if the poach was unsuccessful</u>. If you try for a poach and it doesn't work, *move* back toward the middle and help cover your partner.

Additionally, if you begin to use poaches a lot more in your teamwork, expect the opposing team to react to this accordingly; we've seen over and over again that a strong partner team that uses poaches will incur the other side to start aiming more and more down the middle. This works to the net player's advantage by opening up a lot more opportunities for him or her to smash it into the opponent's side.

CHAPTER FOURTEEN
EQUIPMENT CONSIDERATIONS

Even if you are able to accommodate all of the physical and mental strategies we've discussed so far into your game, at some point your ability to return and actually win against opponents will come down to something external to yourself – namely, what kind of equipment you've got, how well it's suited to your particular body and style, and the sheer quality of it. In tennis, your main piece of equipment is – obviously – going to be what racket you decide to go with. Below we'll go over some of the considerations you should keep in mind while choosing which racket is best for you (size, composition, make, etc.).

Racquets

We generally like to categorize racquets according to size and purpose. The first is the 'Game Improvement Racquets'. These are larger in terms of their heads (107-135 square inches), have a longer grip (27-30 inches) that allows for a more powerful swing arc, and generally around 8-10 ounces. These sorts of rackets are usually preferred by beginners since they are either evenly balanced or have their weight centered more on the head, again to add to the amount of force they can exert on a ball. These racquets tend to favor those with lower and shorter swings since they can still deliver force without sacrificing accuracy or superfluous movement from the player.

The second racquet size and style is tweener and is a good blend of both weight and breadth. They have a 95-100 square inch head, and are generally weighted lighter in the head area, although they do have a longer handle that's around 28 inches. As expected from a racquet that tries to be evenly balanced in all ways, it's a favorite of intermediate players <u>because it offers a higher maneuverability</u> and control of the ball during serves and returns.

The third and final racquet style are control racquets (or 'player racquets'). These are what the professionals tend to go with, and are overall heavier than most other racquets at around 11-13+ ounces. They also have a smaller surface area of 85-95 square inches, meaning that there is less room for error when hitting the ball – however, because they're balanced head-light and inherently low-power, the force must come from the actual player's swing. While this might seem like a trade-off, control racquets have a much thinner arm and are perfectly tempered to maximize their control.

A note on frame stiffness – there is a myth among both beginners and professionals that the stiffness of a racquet, how much it bends or 'gives' upon impact, can deplete energy more if it is stiffer. This is incorrect: a flexible racquet will allow the ball to stay on the strings for anywhere from 2-5 milliseconds, at which point it's depleting more energy than a stiffer racquet. A stiffer racquet supplies more power, but this can also come at the expense of control.

A note on material – just as important as the dimensions of a racquet (and related to the stiffness of the frame) is what the racquet is made of. In the past, most racquets tended to be made of wood, and you can still find some places that specially tailor racquets, but as a general rule of thumb most makers now rely on graphite. Graphite is good because, aside from being cheap, it also has certain physical qualities that make it ideal, including a very light base weight and a powerful energy-rebound ratio (which is why beginner racquets tend to favor this composition). Aluminum is also a common substance. While being even cheaper than graphite, they are a little bit heavier however, although this still makes them a good choice for beginners. For professionals, or those who take the game very seriously, there are also Kevlar and carbon fiber racquets – these are considerably more expensive but offer a much wider variety of control.

String Choice

Just as important as what kind of racquet is the sort of string and its configuration. Strings are made of different materials, and each material has a different effect:

- Nylon – while it is the most inexpensive, it is also the most durable and many off-the-shelf racquets use this as their default. On the downside, it does not cushion very well and can seem very stiff, especially to beginners.

- Nylon/Polyurethane – this blend takes the best of nylon's durability, and blends it with the cushioning factor of polyurethane, giving a much better shock absorption. The one downside of course is that it is much more expensive (upwards of $30+).

- Natural Gut – probably the most expensive on the market, natural gut comes from actual cow intestine. While it gives an unprecedented amount of pop and control, as well as shock absorption, the major downside (other than price) is the fact that it can break very easily if you're not careful.

- Polyester – one of our favorites, it reduces the power (depletes energy) of given shots, but this is often to the advantage of beginners and intermediates because it allows you to put more control on the ball. While still durable, it's not as stiff as nylon and does lose tension quite quickly over time.

- Hybrids – the last sort, this one again tries to blend different elements, and in general has a very good durability; downside again may be the fact that it feels too stiff or 'boardy'.

A note on string density – depending on the racquet, the spaces between the strings may vary according to preference or make; in general the open string configuration helps you put more spin on a ball. For those that have a good slice or topspin serve, having an open racquet can help with those sorts of hits. Conversely, a denser string pattern doesn't grip the ball as well, and is good for those who want to work on ball placement and accuracy via control.

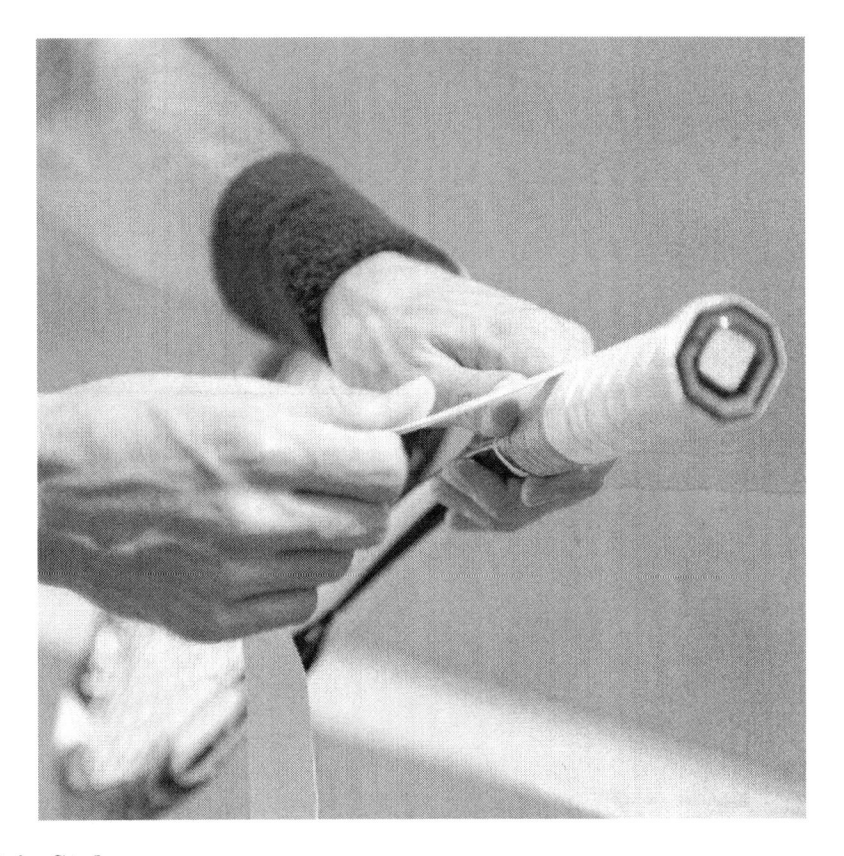

Grip Style

The last detail regarding equipment is the grip – this is essentially the 'handle' of the racquet, and even professionals can sometimes diminish the importance of a grip. This is a huge oversight because the grip is what attaches the racquet (essentially) to your body, so the interface between hand and equipment is understandably important.

Choosing the right grip is, again, often a source of contention among trainers and manuals, but most people agree on a few key measurements – most sizes are between 4 and 4 5/8ths. A personal measurement can be made by measuring from the bottom of the center line in your palm up to the top of your middle finger. Another good method to determine if the racquet grip is the right size is to grip it as you would in your dominant hand. Now, take your index finger on *your other hand* and slide it in between the spaces between your fingers and palm – if there is room for it to fit, then you're probably in the right range.

Vibration Dampeners – essentially, these small devices are usually made of a soft material like rubber. These are placed just below the strings near the throat of the racquet, and their primary function is (as their name suggests) to reduce or ameliorate vibration. However, it should be noted that they <u>only reduce vibration of the strings, not the actual racquet.</u> This has the effect of changing the hard 'pock' sound of impact, and can dampen the auditory feedback of a given hit. In essence, these dampeners can be placed anywhere on the racquet, and come in a variety of forms.

- Worm Dampeners – the one vibration dampener we'd like to look at though is the worm dampener, which (again, as the name suggests) looks like a thin worm that goes across the racquet. This is probably the most common and preferred type of dampener, and will fundamentally change or alter the sound of impact.

- *It should be noted that there is no evidence that vibration dampeners can help with reducing strain from vibrations on a player's actual arm, and do not eliminate or cure common ailments such as tennis elbow or pulled muscles.*

Overgrip – installing an overgrip on your tennis racquet is a good thing to be able to know how to do, especially if you plan on playing tennis a lot. Just like hockey players wrap their sticks with tape to increase friction and their ability to hold onto it, tennis players follow a similar pattern. Using sports tape or medical tape, placing an overgrip means essentially wrapping it to increase your grip on the handle. A few things to keep in mind:

- Face the racquet downward before you begin – if there is already an overgrip you might favor removing it. When wrapping the handle, always do so in a downward direction.

- For right handed players, it's best to go left to right (and vice versa for lefties). When you reach the bottom, take another piece of tape and wrap it straight around to cover the 'bump'.

- Keep it taut! One mistake players often make is not keeping the tension of the tape or wrap, and this can cause bumps or weird overlapping that will pinch or blister your fingers over time.

CHAPTER FIFTEEN
TENNIS PSYCHOLOGY

Throughout the last four chapters, we've covered a lot of the physical aspects of tennis, ranging from strategies you can employ in a singles and doubles game down to the proper choice of equipment. But as we've alluded to – and you've no doubt surmised yourself – there is a huge *mental* component to the sport of tennis as well. The true professional tennis player is one who can operate both on a physical and psychological level. From a psychological point of view, this boils down to two opposing elements: your own ability to interpret the game according to things like how well you respond to certain attacks from an opponent, knowing your limits, and how best to employ them, and being able to interpret your opponent's psychological game as well.

Know Thyself

It might sound like something out of a philosophy textbook, but the concept of having a deep interior knowledge and awareness of yourself has a tremendous effect on well you play against others; for example, being able to humbly accept your weaknesses and strengths goes a long way. Many people either falter too much on one side, by giving themselves too much credit and assuming they are extremely talented at one skillset or another, or not having *enough* confidence, which can have the opposite effect of plunging them into a spiral of low morale and self-esteem.

Weaknesses – everyone has weaknesses in their game to begin, and these are weaknesses that follow us. The sooner you accept these weaknesses and look for ways to overcome them, the quicker you'll see your game improve.

Strengths – we can't stress knowing your strengths enough; however, knowing your strengths is only as effective as being able to utilize them in-game. This is why it's important to have a good strategy in mind that allows you to employ them in a system of movements (i.e. using a topspin serve, following up with good cover down the middle, forcing the left side of the court to prevent backhand strokes).

Know Thy Enemy

Not just good advice from Sun-Tzu, this aphorism applies heavily to tennis as well. As we've seen before, people usually fall somewhere on a spectrum between docile and assertive. The more assertive players tend to gain a lot of ground very quickly on, often forcing the net and attacks, and trying to maintain control of the court. On the other hand, docile players may begin with a strong defense, returning a lot of attacks but never trying to gain a lot of ground. Even as a beginner, you will be able to pick up almost immediately what type your opponent is by how hard, fast, and consistent she meets your serves and returns.

Against Assertive Players – our main tips against playing tough opponents who force the net is to try and capitalize on this assertiveness; most importantly, <u>hold your ground</u>. Don't let them bully you backward, because this will simply give them more ground and space to land winning shots. Instead, use their assertiveness against them by letting them get close – this might involve working on your lob shots to get it over their heads.

Against Docile Players – in general, the competitive nature of tennis means that docile players will routinely have the disadvantage; that doesn't mean they're any easier to play against, however. With a strong defensive edge, it is best to try and vary your approach to docile players – they will most likely be disinclined to use the court to their advantage, so forcing them left and right and back and forth a lot can open up a lot of gaps in their defense.

Controlling the arousal of an enemy is also a key psychological strategy. Depending on the court, there are often tons of variables that are both interior and exterior to the game such as the sound of airplanes or traffic or other people playing in the court next to you. Capitalize on these distractions by observing how your opponent reacts to them.

Confidence

As a wise man once said, confidence can't be taught, it can only be earned. This certainly rings true on the courts, where the feelings someone has can fluctuate almost on the drop of a pin depending on how well he or she can keep up with an opponent. So how does one increase their confidence?

Well, it might seem silly, but vocalizing or emphasizing your strengths in one way or another can have psychological benefits. This might be as simple as having your partner or trainer point out your strengths, or taking things into your hands and writing out your strengths in a journal or on paper – this *self-affirmation*, although tenuous, can be enough to turn your game.

This can also involve visualizing a game where you did very well. Remember how reacted in that game, or better yet, try to envisage your opponent's next hit in the present game. Where do they tend to hit the ball? How would you react? This activity of mental visualization is a useful precursor to a physical reaction – if you're prepared for any contingency *mentally*, then your body has a much easier time reacting and manifesting it *physically*.

Focus and Attention

Related to the idea of 'rhythm' we've already discussed, a player is only 'in his game' when his focus and attention are working together and clarified. There are a few key tips to improving your focus:

- Get Rid Of Limiting Beliefs – this might sound a bit "new age-y" but it has empirical relevance. A person who believes they can win will often have a higher percentage of winning shots, while someone who has already accepted defeat will tend to fall into a self-affirming prophecy. This is probably one of the hardest mental barriers to overcome, but one of the most important, especially for your long game. It is important going into a game against an opponent to believe that you have an adequate chance of defeating him.

- These beliefs can also include certain elements of the game: for example, you might think that you have no chance during a tie, or that your serves are not as good as your opponent's. Eliminating these beliefs is, therefore, crucial; but how do you simply stop believing in these psychic limits? For one, accepting certain things are out of your control can go a long way.

- Don't Deprecate Yourself – even in the best games, you're bound to have ups and downs, where you just can't seem to fall into your rhythm. It is tremendously important not to punish yourself mentally for these small lapses – for one, this leads to more stress, especially if you continue to dwell on the past (what you *should* have done in a given set), and secondly it pulls you out of the moment. Instead, simply brush off a loss of a point – it happened, it's in the past – and focus instead on the present or the future, how to win the next point.

- Trust Your Body – this can also be difficult; while there is a connection between the mind and the body, a lot of tennis players fall into the habit of 'forcing' them to work together, and this usually ends badly. Our bodies, whether we give enough credit to them or not, also operate on a subliminal or subconscious level; instances, where you find yourself reacting without thinking, is a good example. In a no holds barred game of tennis, learning to trust your body on this subconscious level can be the difference between winning or losing. If you have trained yourself physically well, then letting your body <u>react instead of willing it to move</u> can be very beneficial.

- Don't Overthink – in the same vein, a lot of tennis players find themselves racing to come up with a mental strategy, and while there is a need to observe and correlate these observations of your opponent so you can find a way to defeat them, overthinking can slow your reaction time profoundly. Your body will naturally pick up cues from your opponent, and learning to 'empty your mind' and let it respond naturally not only increases your reaction time but also lends itself to a much more fluid playing style.

- Control Emotions – the emotional baseline that you start with at the beginning of a game can also affect your game; for example, if you go into a game happy and energetic, your focus will seem clearer because you're able to put all of your attention into playing. On the other hand, if you have a lot going on in your life – bills, relationships, worries, etc. – these *will* translate into your movements.

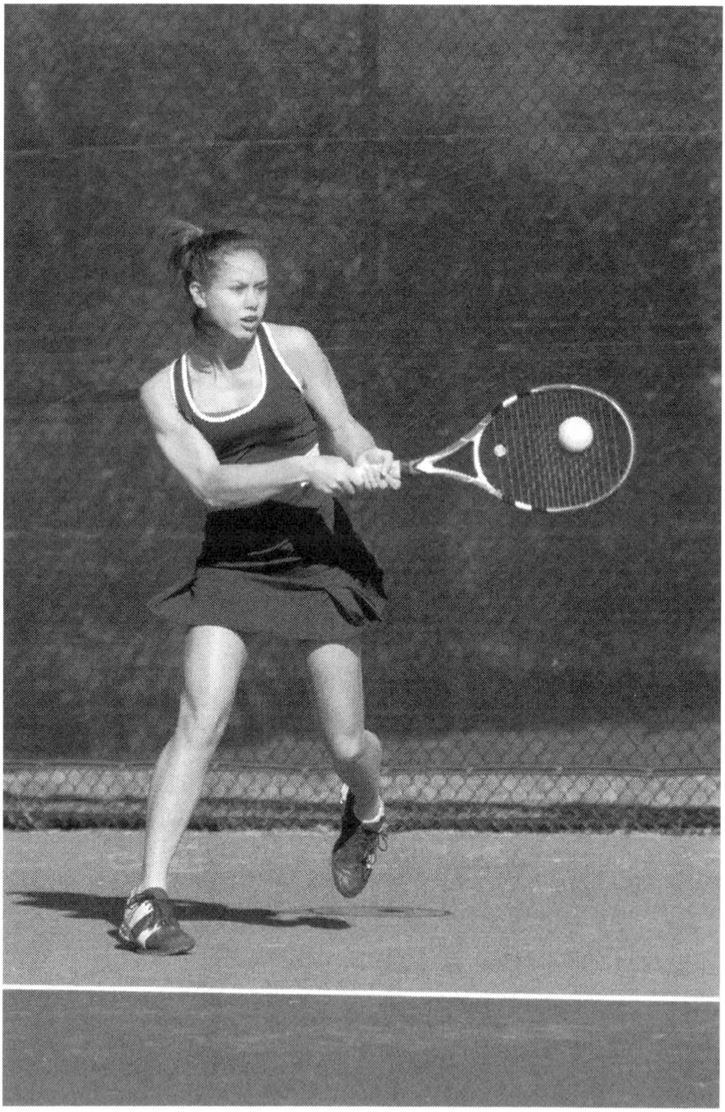

CHAPTER SIXTEEN
DRILL EXERCISES

In this final chapter we address the nitty-gritty application of all the other chapters – basically, you can learn and read as much as you want about tennis and its strategies, but until you *practice* what you've learned it's all for naught. It's the difference between thinking and doing. Regardless of whether you're learning a new sport like tennis or simply trying to improve your game, there is a direct correlation between how well you'll perform on the court and how much time you've dedicated to strengthening your various techniques.

As a result, drill exercises end up being the bend-or-break facet of any tennis player's career, no matter if they're professionals preparing for a big tournament or hobbyists who play once a week with friends. Below we've outlined some of the more important – and we feel salient – drill exercises for improving specific elements of the game such as serves, returns, and cardio fitness.

If you've managed to take anything away from this book so far, it should be that your ability to serve – both in singles and doubles games – accounts for a majority percentage regarding each game's outcome.

1. Our first serving exercise involves splitting your court into three sections – front, middle, and back. Start at the front and try serving 5-10 balls over the net, then back up to the middle and back and repeat. Learning how to instinctively get balls over the next at various incremental distances is vital.

2. With a partner, try the same exercise but work on rallying back and forth. This will accustom you to responding to different shots on different areas of the court (including the amount of power/parabola needed for each attack).

    a. Toss drills – we've also seen that consistency with serves has more to do with the actual toss than necessarily with your ability to hit the ball; in this exercise try tossing the ball up (without hitting it) Toss drills – we've also seen that consistency with serves has more to do with the actual toss than necessarily with your ability to hit the ball; in this exercise try tossing the ball up (without hitting it) Aim for around 7-10 feet, depending on your height. The ball should reach approximately 2 feet over your head at its apex.

    b. It should also be straight up (no arc) and less than 30 centimeters in front of you – the easiest way to check this is to simply throw it up and watch where it lands; adjust as necessary

c. Once you've got a consistent toss get used to hitting the ball – professionals rarely hit at the apex, but wait for the ball to fall a few centimeters. This is all about timing and will vary greatly depending on your back and front swing, as well as your stance.

Pronation Exercises – part of what makes or breaks a good serve is the ability of your arm to properly pronate; this allows for a smooth serve and can help with control, but there are some obvious obstacles that even professionals tend to make and which can be hard to 'unlearn' once they become habits.

- To work on pronation, try this simple exercise – merely throw the ball as you would a baseball; this will help to develop a natural pronation which can translate into your actual serve with a racquet.

- Now try in slow motion using your racquet without a ball – imitate the proper pronation of the wrist and get a feel of how it should feel; practicing swings normally and in slow motion can help you pick out small fluctuations or errors in your swing and allow you to correct them.

- Another good method is to try your serves *without rotating your body* – many beginners and intermediates often over-rotate their body to accommodate a lack of pronation in their wrist. Approach this exercise by using a slice serve, and watch how well you pronate without body rotation.

- Using the index finger – another easy to remember trick that actually works wonders is to focus on the placement of your index finger; after a serve, your index finger should be pointing toward the target you were aiming at (focusing on making sure this is true with every serve will help to instill muscle memory in your wrist's pronation, and also makes for a cleaner hit).

- Be aware of the 'waiters serve' – many people when they are about to serve end up bringing the racquet back so that it is facing the sky, much like a waiter holding up a plate.

    o This can happen for a lot of reasons, but most of it is mental – with an open stance and serve and having the racquet face upward, we naturally think we can hit the ball better

- In many cases we also revert to the waiters serve because we don't trust our pronation; additionally, we might be afraid of accidentally hitting our head

- Lastly, this serve usually develops because we've grown accustomed to a forehand grip and serve and it can be very difficult to overcome the muscle memory attributed to learning the serve this way

Cardio Exercises

Probably the least fun of all the exercises, there is a physical endurance quality to tennis and being able to train the muscle groups related to the sport is something every player should focus on. We will focus on just a few easy exercises that specifically target those muscle groups.

1. Single-Leg Squats – this involves having a bench at about the same height as you would be when sitting; place a pad underneath and with your arms straight out in front of you, try to stand up with both legs, then sit back down. You will feel this pull in the glutes and hamstrings quite

strongly – once you're comfortable with that, try doing it on one leg; lift your left foot off the ground and put all your weight on your right while you stand up.

   a. Some athletes will even try this from a squatting position but requires a lot of strength

2. In order to avoid injury, we also like to work on core strength – the burpee is an excellent way to get your whole body moving and in shape. Start in a standing position, then drop down to a squatting position, place both hands out in front, and raise your hips into the air to create a triangle with your body (some yoga enthusiast might recognize this particular stance); next, jump your legs out behind you so that you are in a push-up position, do a single push-up, and jump back into a crouch position; from here raise your hands above your head, stand up, and do a two-feet standing jump. This exercise works cardio *very hard* and is sure to keep you in physical condition – plus it can be done anywhere!

3. Weighted Pull-up – one of the primary injuries that players experience in tennis is either to their elbow or their shoulder, especially the rotator cuff. Working on muscle groups that help with this movement can stretch out muscles, strengthen them, and help prevent wear and tear – the weighted pull-up involves having a weighted

belt and doing several pull-ups (both anterior and exterior to work the deltoid and biceps).

4. Max distance lateral hop – another good exercise to amp up your cardio is this exercise; balance on one leg, then bend at the knee and leap laterally off of it onto the other leg. You want to absorb as much of the force as possible by bending the knee on your opposite leg and then push off of it. This back and forth will get you sweating in no time but is extremely useful because it helps to mimic the sort of footwork you'd expect from an actual match.

CONCLUSION

The game of tennis isn't just a mindless sport – as we've seen up until now, there is a huge amount of mental and physical components, as well as a very cerebral element to strategy, depending on whether you're playing singles or doubles, or for fun or professionally. It is very much a sport of balance, and when we say that there are several layers. On the surface, being able to incorporate a wide variety of techniques into your game is essential and involves attuning your body to different movements, but this *balance* goes a step further: being able to react quickly to changing situations, the capacity to strategize both in the short and long term, and overcoming your psychological barriers all play a role.

We've focused quite a bit on some of the fundamentals of the game – most notably the single player strategies – such as always aiming "deep and down the middle", and focusing on different serves and how they will affect the outcome (i.e. their advantages and disadvantages). We've also taken an up close and personal look at equipment and how the choice of racquet can affect your game in significant ways. But here we'd also like to reiterate how important the mental aspect of a match is: as much as our performance can be affected negatively or positively by emotions, by our innate confidence and temperament, and by external variables, if you've managed to read this far then we hope you've come to appreciate tennis on a more primal and involved level.

The purpose of this book is to instill in the reader a love for the game, to remind them of the elements that make tennis such a fun and immersive sport, and to hopefully improve their knowledge base and skillset by focusing on both basic and advanced techniques – and analyzing certain common faults, errors, and bad habits that naturally crop up for any player, from the greenest beginner to most seasoned pro. Part of getting better at anything is obviously practice, and using what you've now learned you should see an immediate and positive change in your matches.

But above all, never lose your passion and always remember to have *fun*!

Free Bonus: Get 40% OFF All Of Our Products On Amazon!!

Coupon Code: 21KSport

Checkout Our Tennis Products

http://amzn.to/2fejZeo

http://amzn.to/2fegXXw

Printed in Poland
by Amazon Fulfillment
Poland Sp. z o.o., Wrocław